A GUIDE TO ORTHODOX PSYCHOTHERAPY

---

*The Science, Theology, and Spiritual Practice
Behind It and Its Clinical Applications*

Archbishop Chrysostomos

With a Foreword by Bishop Auxentios

University Press of America,® Inc.
Lanham · Boulder · New York · Toronto · Plymouth, UK

**Copyright © 2007 by
University Press of America,® Inc.**
4501 Forbes Boulevard
Suite 200
Lanham, Maryland 20706
UPA Acquisitions Department (301) 459-3366

Estover Road
Plymouth PL6 7PY
United Kingdom

Library of Congress Control Number: 2006931839
ISBN-13: 978-0-7618-3602-5 (paperback : alk. paper)
ISBN-10: 0-7618-3602-0 (paperback : alk. paper)

⊖™The paper used in this publication meets the minimum
requirements of American National Standard for Information
Sciences—Permanence of Paper for Printed Library Materials,
ANSI Z39.48—1984

Dedication

A man who does not honor his mentors and colleagues dishonors himself. The occasions for showing proper honor and appreciation to those who have helped form me intellectually and spiritually have been few and rare. Therefore, I would like to dedicate this book to them and to take this opportunity to cite a few of them in sequence and by the institutions where—beginning with my first years in university more than four decades ago—I encountered them. This list is not exhaustive by any means, but it *is* representative, honoring both those whom I have mentioned and those whom, for want of space (but not of appreciation), I have not:

At the University of California, **Professor Jeffrey Burton Russell** and **Professor Manfred P. Fleischer,** who opened to me the world of ecclesiastical history and historical theology; at the California State University, **Professor Nikolai E. Khokhlov,** an exemplary mentor, friend, and man of conscience, and **Professor Lee Kalbus,** who helped me to reconcile my interests in science, philosophy, and spirituality; at Princeton University, **Professor John Darley, Professor Joel Cooper,** and the late **Father Georges Florovsky,** who helped, taught, and informed me; at Harvard University, **Andrei Charles Kovacs** and the late **Father Henri Nouwen,** whose friendship and encouragement served—and continue to serve—me well; at Oxford University, **His Grace, Bishop Kallistos of Diokleia,** for his graciousness in hosting me, and **Dr. John V. Petropoulos,** who kindly befriended and helped me; at the Ion Mincu University in Bucharest, Romania, **Professor Augustin Ioan,** my frequent co-author and a source of endless intellectual stimulation; at the University of Washington, Seattle, **Professor Martin S. Jaffee,** a genuine friend who has expanded and refined my spiritual views; at the Graduate Theological Union, Berkeley, the Dean and Vice President for Academic Affairs, the **Reverend Dr. Arthur G. Holder,** for opening to me the scholarly charity of this prestigious institution; and in the proverbial university of life and academy of the soul, **Metropolitan Cyprian of Oropos and Fili,** a genuine man of spirit and my constant rudder and guide in difficult waters.

"Well, as I said, the pilgrim . . . meets this starets—this very advanced religious person. . . . Well, the starets tells him about the Jesus Prayer first of all. 'Lord Jesus Christ. Have mercy on me.' . . . [T]he starets tells the pilgrim that if you keep saying that prayer over and over again—you only have to do it with your *lips* at first—then eventually what happens, the prayer becomes self-active. Something *happens* after a while. . . . [T]he words get synchronized with the person's heartbeats, and then you're actually praying without ceasing. Which has a really tremendous, mystical effect on your whole outlook. I mean that's the whole *point* of it, more or less. I mean you do it to purify your whole outlook and get an absolutely new conception of what everything's about."

Franny and Zooey,
J.D. Salinger

Table of Contents

Foreword

The publication of this volume on Orthodox psychotherapy is a milestone in the development of a body of reliable information in the English language about the Eastern Orthodox understanding of the human person, human psychology, and mental disorders. The millions of Orthodox Christians in the United States and Western Europe and the hundreds of millions of Orthodox worldwide represent what many scholars consider the oldest Christian tradition. Yet, the tragic separation of the Christian East and West in the middle of the eleventh century and the struggles, over many centuries, of Orthodox Christianity in lands beset by invasions and domination by hostile forces—from the conquest of the great Byzantine Empire by the Turks to the fall of the vast Russian Empire and much of Orthodox Eastern Europe to Communism—have led the Western world, until relatively recent times, to forget what some have called the "other half of Christianity." It has also lost cognizance of part of its own Christian heritage. As Western Christianity and the Christian East seek to discover one another again today, small steps have been taken to elucidate the divergent ways in which Orthodox and Western Christians look at the human person and how these different anthropologies touch on the different "psychologies" of the two populations. Here, in his *Guide to Orthodox Psychotherapy*, Archbishop Chrysostomos takes a giant leap forward in this endeavor, providing us with a concise study of the person and psyche from an Eastern Orthodox standpoint and a clear understanding of so-called Orthodox psychotherapy. The likelihood of his book broadening the burgeoning study of the nexus between spirituality and religious beliefs and practices and mental health is great. Its contribution to an appreciation of the importance of cultural and religious diversity in this area of research is immense.

I first encountered Archbishop Chrysostomos' work when he was a layman and doctoral candidate at Princeton University, where I was a student in a preceptorial in personality and Freudian theory taught by him in the department of psychology. I was, at the time, also a student of the late Father Georges Florovsky (1893-1979), who was teaching at Princeton in semi-retirement after a distinguished career as a professor of Eastern Church history and Slavic studies at Harvard University. As a student of mathematics and religion, I was immediately attracted by two traits that both of these individuals exhibited: genius of a rare kind and a profound interest in bringing science and religion into dialogue. Father Florovsky, widely acknowledged as one of the greatest Orthodox theologians of the twentieth century, published his first study, interestingly enough, in the area of physiological psychology. It was presented to the Russian Imperial

Academy of Science by the famous Ivan Pavlov. Archbishop Chrysostomos, like Father Florovsky, also brought together his interest and scientific training in psychology with his earlier graduate study in Byzantine history and his burning interest in the psychology of religion and the role of religious belief in personality formation and its implications for clinical psychology. My initial intellectual formation under the tutelage of these two men has continued through my association with Archbishop Chrysostomos as a colleague in my ecclesiastical vocation and at the Center for Traditionalist Orthodox Studies, where he is a Senior Scholar, and in my intense interest in his publications on psychology and religion, which are redolent with the spirit of Father Florovsky. I have also co-authored a number of books and articles with His Eminence that touch on the interface between science and religion.

This pioneering volume is an outgrowth of Archbishop Chrysostomos' attempt, in a spate of books that have appeared in several languages over the past two and a half decades, to draw from the writings of the Desert Fathers, from the witness of the Greek Church Fathers, and from various Orthodox theological writers what he calls an "Orthodox Patristic psychology"; i.e., an Orthodox view of human psychology consistent with the cosmological and soteriological tenets of Orthodox Christianity. He has also studied the development of Orthodox psychotherapy, to which I referred above, which grew out of an attempt by certain theological circles in the contemporary Greek Church to bring together the mystical Hesychastic teachings of Orthodoxy about the cleansing of the mind by contemplative prayer ("prayer of the heart" or the "Jesus Prayer") and certain spiritual exercises with the methods and goals of psychoanalysis. This effort has now reached beyond the Greek Church to other national Churches and to Orthodox—and not a few non-Orthodox—Christians in the West. In the present book, tying these fascinating developments to the corresponding trend in Western psychiatry and psychology towards a more positive assessment of the effect of religion on mental health, His Eminence presents us with a careful examination of the meeting of religion and psychotherapy as they impact on the Eastern Orthodox Christian specifically and, if not explicitly, at least implicitly on the general population. He is, I must say, one of the few scholars who could have undertaken this kind of study with such success.

The virtual revolution that has taken place in the psychological and psychiatric world with regard to its understanding of the relationship between religion and health and, in particular, religion and mental health makes this book timely. Its emphasis on a largely ignored part of the Christian population, Eastern Orthodox believers, also makes it an absolutely unique and invaluable contribution to the growing literature on religion and mental health. I expect that it will become a standard reference work for psychologists, psychiatrists, and other mental health professionals who are interested in exploring the burning issue of religion and psychotherapy and how it affects a significant and increasingly important, if heretofore often overlooked, segment of the religious population.

Bishop Auxentios, Th.D.

The Right Reverend Dr. Auxentios is Director of the Center for Traditionalist Orthodox Studies and Editor of the periodical Orthodox Tradition.

Acknowledgements

I owe a tremendous debt of gratitude to two men of philanthropy and faithful erudition, whose vision ultimately made possible my research at the Library of Congress, where I wrote the majority of this book: John W. Kluge, who generously funded the Kluge Center, a superb facility for scholarly research and inquiry at the Library, and the late epidemiologist, Dr. David B. Larson, in whose honor the Center's Fellowship in Health and Spirituality was established. I am also profoundly indebted to the Librarian of Congress, Dr. James H. Billington; the kind staff of the Kluge Center (in particular, though not solely, Dr. Prosser Gifford, whose retirement as Director of Scholarly Programs coincided with my appointment as Larson Fellow for the Winter of 2006, his charming successor, Dr. Carolyn Brown, Mary Lou Reker, Special Assistant to the Director, and Robert Saladini, Program Officer); to Dr. Mary-Jane Deeb, Chief of the African and Middle Eastern Division at the Library, and her wonderful and able staff; to Dr. Thomas Mann, Reference Librarian in the Main Reading Room, for his eagerness to help me; to Predrag Paul Pajic, Reference Librarian for South Slavic studies, for his friendship and intelligent reflections; and to the many other individuals who so diligently and indefatigably offered me their invaluable assistance in navigating my way through the extraordinary treasury that is our nation's chief repository for the record of human intellectual achievements.

I must also thank Dr. Ernest Latham, at whose invitation I lectured for the National Foreign Affairs Training Center at the Foreign Service Institute of the U.S. Department of State, during my stay in Washington, D.C., for providing me with intellectual delectation and his warm friendship. Ellen Toomey, who, from retirement, rallied her considerable connections in the U.S. capital to my support, has my fondest gratitude, as well. To Sheilah Kast, the gifted television and radio journalist, for sharing with me her insights and rich experiences, I similarly owe much more than she might imagine. I thank her, too, for the graciousness earlier shown to me (and other Fulbright Scholars in Romania) by her and her husband, James Rosapepe, when he was U.S. Ambassador to that country. Finally, I have no words adequate to express my appreciation to His Grace, Bishop Auxentios of Photiki, who was my research assistant during my appointment at the Kluge Center, and to the brotherhood of the St. Gregory Palamas Monastery and the sisterhood of the Convent of St. Elizabeth the Grand Duchess of Russia, both in Etna, California, for their selfless sacrifices, which made it possible for me to leave my sundry ecclesiastical duties and many personal responsibilities, for a short period of time, in their able hands.

Introduction

What is Orthodox Psychotherapy?

The term "Orthodox psychotherapy" was coined by a gifted religious writer and theologian, Metropolitan Hierotheos Blachos,[1] a clergyman of the Orthodox Church of Greece and Metropolitan of the See of Naupactos (also known as Lepanto, a city of historical importance situated on the Corinthian Gulf in Central Greece). This was the title of his first book about the teachings of the Greek Fathers on the nexus between Orthodox Christian religious practice and mental health, *Orthodoxe Psychotherapeia: Paterike Therapeutike Agoge.*[2] The work appeared in an English translation in 1994 with the title *Orthodox Psychotherapy: The Science of the Fathers.*[3] This first volume was followed, a year later, by a second, *Psychike Astheneia kai Hygeia: Dialogos,*[4] which was translated into English with the title *The Illness and Cure of the Soul in the Orthodox Tradition.*[5] Like the first, Blachos' second book was written before his elevation to the episcopacy. In both of these works, Metropolitan Hierotheos is careful to acknowledge that "the term psychotherapy is relatively new" and that it entails for the psychologist or psychiatrist an "anthropology which differs from the anthro-

---

1. Here I have used, as I will throughout this book, the classical system of transliteration for Greek words, including proper names and place names, except when quoting materials or publication data which follow one of the several alternative systems used in the transliteration of modern Greek. Hence, for example, the divergence between the classical rendering "Blachos" and the alternative "Vlachos."

2. Archimandrite Hierotheos Blachos, *Orthodoxe Psychotherapeia: Paterike Therapeutike Agoge* (Orthodox psychotherapy: A patristic therapeutic regimen) (Edessa, Greece: Hiera Mone Timiou Staurou, 1986). I have translated the Greek word *"agoge"* as regimen; the reference here is, of course, to the classical *agoge*, or the educational and training regimen for young boys in ancient Sparta.

3. Bishop of Nafpaktos Hierotheos, *Orthodox Psychotherapy: The Science of the Fathers*, trans. Esther Williams (Levadia, Greece: Birth of the Theotokos Monastery, 1994). This English translation is unfortunately of uneven accuracy and at times stilted in style.

4. Archimandrite Hierotheos Blachos, *Psychike Astheneia kai Hygeia: Dialogos* (The sickness and health of the soul: A dialogue) (Lebadeia, Greece: Hiera Mone Genethliou tes Theotokou, 1987).

5. Archimandrite Hierotheos Vlachos, *The Illness and Cure of the Soul in the Orthodox Tradition*, trans. Effie Mavromichali (Levadia, Greece: Birth of the Theotokos Monastery, 1993).

pology and soteriology of the Church Fathers."[6] "Psychology as a science," he observes, is a modern discipline, which he considers a "fruit" of Western Christianity and not the Greek Patristic tradition.[7] Nonetheless, despite those points at which modern psychology comes into conflict with Greek Patristic teachings, he argues that in many instances the former is "in agreement" with the latter.[8] In fact, almost a decade after the publication of the two aforementioned books, Metropolitan Hierotheos undertook the publication of a fascinating work comparing Orthodox psychotherapy and the psychoanalytical precepts of Viktor Frankl's Logotherapy, in which he says that Frankl's concern about the lack of meaning in the life of the contemporary human is a "common point" of contact with Orthodox psychotherapy.[9]

The impact of Metropolitan Hierotheos' books on the dialogue between theology and the mental health professions in Greece was not immediate. But about the time that they began to appear in English translation in the West, his ideas were coming to be widely debated in Greek intellectual circles. Though his writings provoked some strong opposition from various detractors, he was in general credited with generating a debate about religion and mental health and, as one Greek physician and religious writer describes them, a "marvelous series" of books "on Orthodox psychotherapy."[10] The appearance of his volumes in the English-speaking West—where, as an Orthodox Christian counselor recently wrote, there has been "increasing interest" in the "relationship between spirituality and health"[11]—sparked an immediate outburst of enthusiasm among Orthodox believers and numerous non-Orthodox believers and scholars familiar with Orthodox studies. This sudden interest in Orthodox psychotherapy also helped thrust into the limelight some of my own work, which I initiated just several years before Metropolitan Hierotheos' writings about Orthodoxy and psychol-

---

6. Blachos, *Orthodoxe Psychotherapeia*, p. 15. Unless otherwise noted, quoted passages from this and other Greek sources, or from sources in other non-English languages, are my own translations from the original text.

7. Blachos, *Psychike Astheneia*, p. 50.

8. Blachos, *Orthodoxe Psychotherapeia*, p. 15.

9. Metropolitan Hierotheos of Naupactos and St. Blaise, *Hyparxiake Psychologia kai Orthodoxe Psychotherapeia* (Existential psychology and orthodox psychotherapy), 2nd ed. (Lebadeia: Hiera Mone Genethliou tes Theotokou, 1997), p. 122.

10. Soteres K. Adamides, M.D., Ph.D., *Therapeutike ton Pateron kai Psychoanalyse* (The therapeutics of the fathers and psychoanalysis) (Athens: Ekdoseis A.E. Stamoules, 2002), p. 38.

11. Stephen Muse, Introduction to *Raising Lazarus: Integral Healing in Orthodox Christianity*, ed. Stephen Muse (Brookline, MA: Holy Cross Orthodox Press, 2004), p. 3.

ogy were published in Greece. My research has been centered not so much on the techniques of spiritual and psychological healing in Orthodox spiritual practice (though a few of my writings have certainly touched on that subject) as on an endeavor to establish an "Orthodox Patristic psychology"; that is, a statement about human cognition, social psychological factors in human behavior, human sexuality, and abnormal psychology as seen through the prism of the teachings of the Desert Fathers (the monastic hermits of the Desert, who flourished in the deserts of Syria, Egypt, and Palestine roughly from the late third well into the sixth century) and the broader Greek Patristic witness. Nonetheless, the complementary nature of our work was obvious, and my work has often been included, along with that of Metropolitan Hierotheos, under the umbrella of Orthodox psychotherapy.

In 2000, much to my surprise and pleasure, the American Psychological Association, in an important attempt to bring religious issues and traditions to the attention of psychotherapists, included in its *Handbook of Psychotherapy and Religious Diversity*[12] a chapter on psychotherapy with Eastern Orthodox Christians. With this effort to encourage "mental health professionals to acquire greater competency in religious and spiritual aspects of diversity,"[13] the APA brought further attention to Orthodox psychotherapy, with the citation of Metropolitan Hierotheos' books and several of my own. In reference to this, an Orthodox scholar recently wrote that

> Orthodox psychotherapy and . . . [Archbishop Chrysostomos'] . . . work have gained national recognition by mental health professionals. In 2002 [*sic*], for example, the American Psychological Association published its *Handbook of Psychotherapy and Religious Diversity*, containing a rare chapter—one of the first of its kind—by clinical psychologist T.R. Young on the treatment of Orthodox Christians suffering from psychological disorders ('Psychotherapy with Eastern Orthodox Christians'). In his commentary, the author notes that 'two recent writers have done extensive work in the psychology of the Fathers of the Orthodox Faith which relates either to the psychology of spiritual development or to Orthodox practice as therapy': specifically, 'Archbishop Chrysostomos of Etna and Archimandrite [now Metropolitan] Hierotheos Vlachos' (p. 110).
>
> Dr. Young goes on to list and summarize, in addition to Metropolitan Hierotheos' numerous and influential books on Orthodox psychotherapy . . . , the four small volumes—three of them co-authored—in Archbishop Chrysostomos' pioneering series, *Themes in Orthodox Patristic Psychology*. Drawing on

---

12. P. Scott Richards and Allen E. Bergin, eds., *Handbook of Psychotherapy and Religious Diversity* (Washington, DC: American Psychological Association, 2000).

13. *Ibid.*, p. 5.

these sources, Young concludes that the Orthodox spiritual life has, as its 'penultimate goal,' the 'cure of the passions . . . , their transformation,' and a consequent 'communion with God' (p. 102). In this succinct synopsis, he brings together the dominant themes in His Eminence's four books (and a number of his other publications in pastoral psychology) . . . [and] . . . the complementary writings of Metropolitan Hierotheos.[14]

In addition to bringing to the attention of mental health professionals the idea of Orthodox psychotherapy and its fundamental notions about the cure and transformation of the passions (emotions) as a path to communion with God and the restoration of the human being to healthful soundness, Young carefully sets forth many of the religious practices of the Orthodox Church. In so doing, he points out that even if "virtually any psychological intervention would be all right to use with the majority of Orthodox persons, . . . most Orthodox will not respond well to spiritual interventions in psychotherapy and counseling," since "many, if not most, Orthodox clients will have spoken with their priest about their psychological problems before making an appointment with a therapist." The priest, he observes, will probably have already offered guidance on "both the psychological and spiritual aspects of the problem."[15] It is important to understand that, in making these points, Young brings into focus the fact that the practice of the Orthodox Christian religion assumes a relationship between the spiritual and psychological life. This helps further to explain how Orthodox psychotherapy so quickly gained the attention of Orthodox Christians and why, to some extent, "Orthodox clergy are open and willing to work with psychotherapists."[16]

There is no doubt, then, that Orthodox psychotherapy and what I have called Orthodox Patristic psychology have come into their own, both in Greece, where Metropolitan Hierotheos' writings have brought the idea to the attention of theological and medical circles, and, with markedly greater fanfare, in the West—and the United States in particular. In fact, a number of books using "Orthodox psychotherapy" in their titles have appeared in the last five years or so throughout the Orthodox world. One example of such is an "e-book" by the Russian psychiatrist D.A. Avdeev, in which the author discusses the role of

---

14. Bishop Auxentios of Photiki, "Notes on Pastoral Psychology," *Orthodox Tradition,* Vol. 23, no. 1 (2006), p. 7.

15. Tony R. Young, "Psychotherapy with Eastern Orthodox Christians," chapter 4 in *Handbook of Psychotherapy and Religious Diversity,* ed. P. Scott Richards and Allen E. Bergin (Washington, DC: American Psychological Association, 2000), pp. 102-103.

16. *Ibid.,* p. 103.

spiritual malaise and the passions and virtues in the etiology and treatment of a variety of mental disorders, as well as the importance of the priest, in coopera- tion with a psychologist or psychiatrist, in helping to "reinstate the correct spiri- tual sensation of life"[17] in a patient. He also places great emphasis on the need for repentance, fasting, prayer, and general participation in religious activities in his advocacy of Orthodox psychotherapy.[18] In addition to the increased availabi- lity of books about Orthodox psychotherapy, a few counseling centers purport- ing to incorporate Orthodox psychotherapy, in one form or another, into their treatment methods have sprung up in the U.S. and Canada.[19] However, despite the interest in and enthusiasm about Orthodox psychotherapy, the proliferation of publications about it, and its nascent emergence as a putative therapeutic method, there has been to date no systematic study of the subject. If we can now generally define and identify Orthodoxy psychotherapy, the need still remains 1) to place it in the context of the broader scientific study of religion and mental health; 2) to examine its theological antecedents and presuppositions; and 3) to define what its specific method of treatment entails and to evaluate the potential effectiveness of that treatment in its clinical application. This study intends to do just that, for the first time providing psychologists and psychiatrists, other men- tal health professionals, and the interested layman with a concise summary and evaluation of Orthodox psychotherapy and a critical guide to what it has to offer the Orthodox Christian and, in the service of diversity, the non-Orthodox and the non-believer alike.

---

17. D.A. Avdeev, *Orthodox Psychotherapy,* trans. Nicolas and Natalie Semyanko, Missionary Leaflet # E142 (La Cañada, CA: Holy Trinity Mission, 2004) (http://www.fat heralexander.org/booklets/english/orthodox_psychotherapy_d_avdeev_e.htm), p. 52. (Ac- cessed January 3, 2006.)

18. *Ibid.,* pp. 25-26 *pass.*

19. One such center is the Therapia Psychotherapy Services in Bethesda, Maryland, which provides, in addition to its own counseling services, referrals to Orthodox counsel- ors in Arizona, Georgia, South Carolina, and Ottawa, Canada.

Chapter I

Science and the Relationship Between Religious Practice and Mental Health

> "You may promise yourself everything—but health, without which there is no happiness. An attention to health then should take place of every other object." *Thomas Jefferson*[20]

Though "[r]eligion has been one of the most important forces throughout human history," as Harold Pincus, Deputy Medical Director of the Office of Research of the American Psychiatric Association, wrote in 1998, "the medical and mental health professions have generally not acknowledged that power."[21] Indeed, cultural sociologist and social critic Frank Furedi has observed (like others) that both in the United States and the United Kingdom there seems to be "a potent mood of intolerance towards expressions of religious faith in popular culture today."[22] That this anti-religious tendency extends at times beyond popular culture to science is clearly illustrated by the protests leading up to a keynote address by the Tibetan Dalai Lama on meditation and neuroscience at the annual meeting of the Society for Neuroscience in Washington, D.C., on November 12, 2005. A significant and vocal contingent of the some 37,000 members of this prestigious scientific organization signed a petition objecting to the religious leader's presence at that event. As Dr. Jianguo Gu, a neuroscientist at the University of Florida, candidly put it, "I don't think that it's appropriate to have a prominent religious leader at a scientific event."[23] Nonetheless, over the past decade or so, we have also seen a strong and significant counter-trend to scienti-

20. Thomas Jefferson, "Letter to Thomas Mann Randolph, Jr., July 6, 1787," in *The Papers of Thomas Jefferson,* ed. Julian P. Bond (Princeton, NJ: Princeton University Press, 1955), Vol. 11, p. 558.

21. Harold Alan Pincus, M.D., in the Preface to *Handbook of Religion and Mental Health,* ed. Harold G. Koenig (San Diego, CA: Academic Press, 1998), p. xxv.

22. Frank Furedi, "Anti-Religious Hysteria" (online essay, 1/26/2006), *Spiked* (London: Signet House) (http://www.spiked-online.com). Accessed January 24, 2006.

23. David Adam, "Plan for Dalai Lama Lecture Angers Neuroscientists," *The Guardian,* July 27, 2005, p. 8.

fic indifference or hostility towards religious belief and practice. This can be attributed to a number of factors, I believe, including, in part, very deliberate attempts by a number of indefatigable pioneers in the health sciences—and especially psychology and psychiatry—to bring medicine and religion into serious dialogue.

Of primary importance among the factors that have helped to curb the growth of negative attitudes towards religion among scientists is the fact that cultural "moods" are not universal. Even in periods that have been characterized by historians and sociologists as "less religious" or more inimical to religious belief and practice than others, there were always intensely religious people—many of these among the most prominent intellectuals and scientists of their age—who acknowledged the beneficial aspects of religion. This was true even of such supposed nemeses of religion as Charles Darwin or, in more recent times, Albert Einstein, both of whom actually praised religion in its salutary expression. Moreover, human beings tend to be pragmatic. If, as Jefferson contends in the excerpt from one of his letters that introduces this chapter, health takes priority over all other human interests, it stands to reason that to the extent that religion can be demonstrated to benefit a person's health, whether mental or physical, indifference and hostility towards it will either significantly wane or, at the very least, prove themselves less effective in discouraging religious belief and practice. Therefore, at a time when "researchers have identified effects of religious involvement on many mental and physical health outcomes" that are "mostly salutary,"[24] as Jeffrey Levin and Linda Chatters, researchers from the National Institute for Health Care Research and the University of Michigan at Ann Arbor, respectively, have averred, those already well-disposed towards religion and those with a pragmatic eye towards health issues are frequently found in the same camp.

Religion and Medical Science
Seeking Common Ground

The evidence and data emerging from efforts within that camp help to explain how, over a short period of time that corresponds almost precisely to the period in which we have seen the flowering of interest in Orthodox psychother-

---

24. Jeffrey S. Levin and Linda M. Chatters, "Research on Religion and Mental Health: An Overview of Empirical Findings and Theoretical Issues," chapter 3 in *Handbook of Religion and Mental Health,* ed. Harold G. Koenig (San Diego, CA: Academic Press, 1998), p. 37.

apy, science and religion are forging a new alliance of sorts. This alliance has challenged the idea that the two fields have nothing in common or that a dialogue between scientists and religious figures is "inappropriate." For well over a decade, as I noted above, significant articles and books have investigated and evaluated the effects of religious belief and practice on physical and mental health. Prominent among those responsible for generating this important body of literature is a group of scientists from Duke University (often referred to as the "Duke Doctors"), who have worked assiduously to compile systematic assessments of the relationship between religion and health—and again, though not exclusively, mental health in particular. This Duke connection is not, of course, adventitious, since both the psychology department, which in the 1950s and 1960s sponsored the parapsychological work of J.B. Rhine, and the medical school at this prestigious learning center have consistently been in the vanguard of avant-garde research and supportive of interdisciplinary studies. It is not surprising, therefore, that two of the authors of one of the foundational works on the nexus between religion and the health sciences, the *Handbook of Religion and Health*,[25] which appeared in 2001, were health professionals associated with Duke University: Harold Koenig, a professor of psychiatry and Director of the university's Center for Spirituality, Theology and Health, and the late David B. Larson, adjunct professor of psychiatry and behavioral science at Duke. Together with psychologist Michael McCullough of Miami University, they produced a book that in many ways set the standards for subsequent investigations in the field. In discussing Orthodox psychotherapy, I will draw heavily from their observations.

The Legacy of a Culture of Disengagement Between Religion and the Health Sciences

In order to understand the truly revolutionary nature of this new courtship between religion and the medical sciences, it behooves us to reflect a bit further on how entrenched anti-religious sentiments have been, heretofore, in the health sciences. Inarguably, the mood of intolerance towards religion that cultural observers see in contemporary Western society is nothing new; it has been part of the intellectual fabric of the so-called Christian West for many centuries, rising and falling in popularity and influence according to the vicissitudes of popular culture. In the health professions, this intolerance has always had its fervent ad-

---

25. Harold G. Koenig, M.D., Michael E. McCullough, Ph.D., David B. Larson, M.D., *Handbook of Religion and Health* (New York: Oxford University Press, 2001).

vocates, fostering a tendency, among a significant portion of medical professionals, to dismiss religion as superstition. Psychology and psychiatry, in particular, have long entertained the idea that there is a ubiquitous pathological
element in religion and in religious figures. This idea is deeply rooted in our
culture. Let me, for example, bring to memory the American poet and novelist
Clement Wood (1888-1950). Most standard anthologies of poetry contain his
works, and his close association with Upton Sinclair, a short stint as an instruc-
tor in poetry at New York University, and a successful career in law (in his na-
tive Alabama, he held a prominent judicial appointment once held by Justice
Hugo Black) make him a singularly gifted figure in the ranks of the American
intelligentsia. His impact on a number of celebrated American thinkers in areas
as diverse as literature, law, and sociology can be measured by the remarkable
extent to which his ideas and sometimes-iconoclastic views are reflected in their
writings and ruminations. Though his reflections on psychology and behavior
are by no means well known, Wood was also an amateur psychoanalyst, direct-
ing his self-appointed eminence in this avocation to such studies as *How to Psycho-Analyze Your Neighbors*[26] and *A Psycho-Analysis of Jesus*.[27] This latter
work, though seldom cited or acknowledged, had, in fact, a tremendous influence on the thinking of his peers and on psychologists and psychiatrists in his
day. This influence can still be seen in what is very often a rather presumptuous
and questionable misuse of psychoanalytical theory in the service of raw anti-religious sentiment, for which he is in no small way responsible.

Wood's assessment of the life of Jesus Christ is one that sounds all too familiar to anyone accustomed to hearing one of the more popular mantras of
those who believe that the negative impact of contemporary religious belief and
practice derives ultimately from the psychopathology of the historical founders
of the world's major religions. Though admitting with some admiration that He
was a "genuine poet," Wood claims that Christ's "conception of love had been
twisted to an anti-human torment by an emotional flood of passion for his mother."[28] To support this supposition, he turns to evidence from a number of religious texts of apocryphal provenance that circulated at the time that the early
Christian Church was struggling to establish and promulgate what it considered
a more accurate canon of Scripture. This canon, reflecting the mainstream and
consensual beliefs about the life of Christ that had survived in oral and written

---

26. Clement Wood, *How to Psycho-Analyze Your Neighbors* (Girard, KS: Haldemann-
Julius Co., n.d.) (Little Blue Book #1344).

27. Clement Wood, *A Psycho-analysis of Jesus* (Girard, KS: Haldemann-Julius Co.,
1926) (Little Blue Book #1071).

28. *Ibid.*, p. 57.

form, Wood rejects as incomplete, contrived, and misleading. In a full-blown diagnosis of Jesus as a classical example of someone whose ethical, sexual, and social ideas were influenced by an overweening attachment to his mother, Wood summarizes Christ's religious motives by opining that they "lay in his subjection to an over affection for his mother, designated by modern psychology as the Oedipus complex."[29] In a leap from diagnosing the ills of its founder to decrying the pejorative philosophical and social consequences of Christianity for society in general, he celebrates what he saw in his time as "Europe's mood against the Christian shackles" restricting its evolution, "as the Christian myth struggles palely in its death throes."[30] It was, of course, his implicit wish that American society would eventually free itself from similar intellectual fetters.[31]

Overcoming Past Prejudices on Newly-Found Common Ground

In the face of such undercurrents of thought about the pathological roots of religion and a general disdain for spiritual pursuits, and in the light of a purported resurgence of anti-religious sentiments in Great Britain and America, a rapprochement between religion and science in the field of medicine can only be called extraordinarily remarkable. But the roots of this unwonted engagement have actually been widespread, reaching into the fertile intellectual soil of unlikely places. Eugene Webb, in his fascinating study of intellectual trends in contemporary France, reminds us, for example, that after its own social upheavals in the late 1960s and the fall of communism in Eastern Europe in the 1980s and '90s, there was a rebirth of interest in religion among that country's notoriously secular scholarly illuminati:

> [Jean-Paul] Sartre's communist phase is well known in the English-speaking world . . . , but few know that he spent the last years of his life in the study of

---

29. *Ibid.*, p. 62.

30. *Ibid.*, p. 64.

31. It is not my purpose to enter into fray about just *how religious* the American public is or is not; however, despite Wood's wish and Professor Furedi's observations about an anti-religious mood in Great Britain and America, polls seem to suggest that religious practice is widespread in this country. According to a survey of religious attendance in the U.S., conducted by Mitofsky and Edison Media Research for *Religion and Ethics Newsweekly* and *U.S. News and World Report* in 2002, 47% of those surveyed reported attending religious services at least once a week (http://www.pbs.org/wnet/religionandeth ics/week534/specialreport.html). Accessed January 30, 2006.

the Old Testament. Julia Kristeva has become known in this country [the U.S.] as a leading French feminist, but relatively few realize that she is also a convert to Catholicism whose writings on the problem of our relation to alterity also express a strong interest in the theological dimension of that theme.[32]

This was also a trend in other European countries at the time, not only among philosophers and social activists, but in scientific circles as well. And though as late as the 1970s, as Susan Larson noted in a festschrift published in honor of her late husband in 2004, "the prevailing theory" among most mental health professionals in this country (and to a large extent abroad) was still "that religion was preponderantly detrimental to mental health,"[33] changes were in the making. And these changes, as I have observed, had a great deal to do with research undertaken by her husband and others. Speaking of her husband's research, Mrs. Larson says that, after a "systematic review of all quantitative articles published in 1978-1989 in the *American Journal of Psychiatry* and *Archives of General Psychiatry*," he found that "a large majority of articles—around 80 percent—indicated a positive clinical association between spirituality/religion[34] and better

---

32. Eugene Webb, *The Self Between: From Freud to the New Social Psychology of France* (Seattle and London: University of Washington Press, 1993), p. 247.

33. Susan S. Larson, "The Nearly Forgotten Factor in Psychiatry: What a Difference a Decade Makes: The Twentieth Annual Oskar Pfister Award Address," chapter 4 in *Faith, Medicine, and Science: A Festschrift in Honor of Dr. David B. Larson*, ed. Jeff Levin and Harold G. Koenig (New York: The Haworth Pastoral Press, 2004), p. 85.

34. In their *Handbook of Religion and Health* (*op. cit.*), Koenig *et al.* make a distinction between religion and spirituality. Religion they define as "an organized set of beliefs, practices, rituals and symbols" that allows an individual to access the sacred (God, ultimate reality, the transcendent, etc.) *and* to develop and further his "relationship and responsibility to others in living together in a community." Spirituality they define as one's personal quest for, or encounter with, the sacred and "ultimate questions about life, about meaning, and about relationship to the sacred or transcendent." Spirituality, they point out, "may (or may not) lead to or arise from the development of religious rituals and the formation of community" (p. 18). In general, throughout this work I prefer to subsume the idea of spirituality under the term religion, unless a specific distinction between the two is indicated. In so doing, I follow the brilliantly comprehensive definition of religion offered by the historian of religion Martin Jaffee: "Religion is an intense and sustained cultivation of a style of life that heightens human awareness of morally binding connections between the self, the human community, and the most essential structures of reality. Religions posit various orders of reality and help individuals and groups to negotiate their relations with these orders." Professor Jaffee's definition, it seems to me, captures the distinction between religion and spirituality, while still allowing one to use the word "re-

mental health. A much smaller proportion of the research found negative associations." He discovered, she goes on to say, that "a patient's spirituality and religion were complex, potentially beneficial at times, and not necessarily harmful. In fact, associations with mental health benefits were far more frequent than associations with harm."[35]

A Systematic Assessment of Religion and Mental Health

When, in 2001, Drs. Koenig, McCullough, and Larson published their *Handbook of Religion and Health,* a book which I have described as having in many ways set the standards for subsequent investigations of the nexus between religion and health, they brought under careful scrutiny all of those factors which, in the past, contributed to the often hostile alienation of science and religion and the empirical data and new attitudes that have facilitated a rapprochement between the two fields. Though my specific interest in this work is focused on the authors' comments and findings about religion and mental health in particular, let me first say something about the conceptual framework of their research and, of course, something about their observations regarding the relationship between religious beliefs and practices and health in general.

Two of the authors of the *Handbook of Religion and Health,* Larson and McCullough, and psychologist Everett L. Worthington, from Virginia Commonwealth University, have set forth, in another scholarly publication, the conceptual framework that underlies their approach to the scientific study of religion or spirituality and mental health, a field that they acknowledge to be "fraught with philosophical and emotional challenges."[36] The first principle that they point out is that

---

ligion" in a more encompassing manner. (See Martin S. Jaffee, *Early Judaism* [Upper Saddle River, NJ: Prentice Hall, 1997], p. 5.) Dale Cannon, in his book on the dimensions of comparative religion, *Six Ways of Being Religious* (Belmont, CA: Wadsworth Publishing Company, 1996), also employs the term "religion" in a comprehensive way. He argues that some conception of an "ultimate reality . . . is generic to all religion," regardless of the differences in what he calls the "outward forms" of religious practice (p. 22).

35. Larson, "Forgotten Factor," p. 86.

36. Michael E. McCullough, David B. Larson, and Everett L. Worthington, in the Introduction to "Mental Health," Section 4 in *Scientific Research on Spirituality and Health,* ed. David B. Larson, M.D., M.S.P.H., James Swyers, M.A., and Michael E. McCullough, Ph.D. (Rockville, MD: National Institute for Health Research, 1998), p. 56.

scholars who study religion and spirituality must walk a fine line between scientific reductionism and religious triumphalism. On the one hand, scientists try
to understand complex phenomena by 'reducing' them to less complex principles. Although the scientific study of religion and spirituality has inherited this
reductionist approach, it is necessary to eschew scientific work that seeks merely to demonstrate that spirituality and religion are 'nothing more' than nervous
system processes, a means to fill some primitive psychological needs, or other
reductionist explanations. . . . Researchers in this field must also eschew scientific work that seeks to promote a particular religion or spiritual agenda.[37]

Adherence to this principle greatly enhances the objective quality and scientific
value of the *Handbook of Religion and Health.* So, too, does the tacit restate-
ment, in a number of instances, of the following conceptual principle, which I
take as an endorsement of my attempt to discuss Orthodox psychotherapy within
its peculiar theological antecedents and presuppositions; i.e., within the "spiritual culture" of the Christian East and its cosmological, anthropological, and
soteriological traditions:

[I]t is crucial to acknowledge that the way one defines mental health varies
from culture to culture, and that some definitions of mental health would not be
acceptable to members of different world religions. . . . [W]e also acknowledge
that we are primarily from Western traditions, although we represent a wide variety of religious affiliations (as well as atheistic and agnostic perspectives).
Thus, our definition of mental health is distinctly Western. . . . As we discuss
how scientific progress can be made in the study of the relationship between
spirituality, religion, and mental health, we recognize that our implicit definitions of mental health should be continually examined so that their cultural context can be appreciated.[38]

In keeping with their objective approach, the authors of the *Handbook of
Religion and Health* also candidly concede that "certain religious beliefs can in-
terfere with the timely seeking of medical care and may delay diagnosis and
treatment, leading to worse health outcomes." This occurs because

religious beliefs may prevent sufferers from complying with medical treatments
by encouraging them to rely on faith rather than on traditional medical care;
they may therefore refuse potentially life-saving blood transfusions, prenatal
care, childhood vaccinations, or other standard treatments or prevention meas-

---

37. *Ibid.*
38. *Ibid.*

ures.[39]

They likewise concede that mental patients who "present with bizarre and distorted religious ideas" or who use "religious beliefs and practices" in "pathological ways" surely suffer negatively on account of their religious beliefs or practices.[40] Nonetheless, they argue, with regard to the positive effects of religion on general health, "[I]t is clear that much of the general public and a growing number of health professionals believe that religion and good health are somehow related."[41] Moreover, they add, "the claims of religious abuse and negative effects of religion on health rest largely on isolated case reports and highly selected case theories, rather than on population-based systematic research studies."[42] Once more, though "some religious attitudes are associated with worse health outcomes,"[43] and allowing that "[r]eligious and health professionals may debate the benefits or risk to health that religion conveys," it still remains that

> people with serious health problems, people fighting against life-threatening or life-disabling diseases, tell us the most about how religion relates to health. Even if no relationship existed, religion would be relevant to health care if patients perceived that it improved their coping with health problems and therefore wished health care providers to address spiritual issues as part of their medical or psychiatric care.[44]

After a careful analysis and critical review of more than 1,600 studies and commentaries on the relation between religion and physical and mental health, Koenig, McCullough, and Larson conclude that the "tools of the clergy's trade—prayer, a trusting faith, inspirational Scripture, powerful ritual, supportive community—may have important influences on mental and physical health. . . . Effective treatment, in fact, may require a spiritual dimension of care."[45] Their findings provide puissant support for the idea that a meeting of religion and the health sciences is not only appropriate but perhaps vital.

Concerning religion and mental health specifically, the authors of the *Handbook of Religion and Health* faced, in their analytical and critical investigation of the literature in the area, not only an historical legacy from the disengagement

39. Koenig *et. al., Handbook of Religion and Health*, p. 77.
40. *Ibid.*
41. *Ibid.*, p. 59.
42. *Ibid.*, p. 77.
43. *Ibid.*, p. 94.
44. *Ibid.*, p. 78.
45. *Ibid.*, p. 449.

of religion and the mental health professions and the prejudices which it spawn-
ed; they were also forced to confront the fact that these prejudices are reinforced
by what is frequently taken as a direct correlation between religious experiences
and some forms of mental illness. "Mental illnesses . . . can be accompanied by
bizarre religious delusions,"[46] as they remark, a possibility that suggests to the
casual observer, if not a causal-effectual relationship, at the very least a compelling association of seemingly more than incidental significance that easily succumbs to a notion of causality:

> [T]he textbook of psychiatric nomenclature and categorization, the Diagnostic
> and Statistical Manual of Mental Disorders (DSM), has for years used religious
> examples to illustrate cases of serious mental illness. . . . While such references
> have been removed from DSM-IV [the latest edition of the *Manual*[47]] in an ef-
> fort to be culturally sensitive, this underscores the point that religious beliefs
> and experiences often accompany mental illness.[48]

Ad finem fidelis to the "old school" of pitting religion against science, many a
mental health professional has tenaciously held to negative ideas of religion because such

> views . . . are to a large extent based on personal belief, opinion, and clinical
> experience working with mentally ill patients, rather than on systematic re-
> search. While it is evident to many that bias plays a strong role in the [positive]
> views of religious professionals and religious health professionals [towards re-
> ligion], less easily recognized is the fact that bias also plays a strong role in the
> [negative] perspective of the secular health professionals.[49]

---

46. *Ibid.,* p. 71.

47. Though "cultural sensitivities" and "political correctness" have, indeed, influenced
entries in the DSM-IV, it is still the case that religion and delusion are clearly associated
with one another. Under "297.1 Delusional Disorders," we find, for example, that the
subtype "Grandiose Type" delusion "may have a religious content (e.g., the person be-
lieves that he or she has a special message from a deity)." Needless to say, without careful elucidations and equivocations one might easily conclude, along with Clement Wood
(*vide supra*), that every religious leader with a claim to a mission or "calling" from God
is delusional. (See the *Diagnostic and Statistical Manual of Mental Disorders,* 4th edition, second printing [Washington, DC: American Psychiatric Association, 1995], p.
297.)

48. Koenig *et al., Handbook of Religion and Health,* p. 71.

49. *Ibid.*

It is, as the authors remark, "not surprising that mental health professionals have often concluded that religious beliefs and practices have a negative impact on mental health, particularly when many of their patients express religious ideas." However, while such conclusions may be understandable, they are not supported by the literature that the authors of the *Handbook of Religion and Health* review and analyze. Neither, at the same time, is the assumption that "religious beliefs and practices actually cause mental illness, or are the result of mental illness" one which the data presented in their book support. In the end, such an assumption, as the authors generously allow, "remains a subject of debate."[50]

Beyond the issue of causality *per se*, the notion of a close connection between religion and mental illness—the former as a cause of the latter *or* the latter as a cause of the former—has its roots, again, partly in psychoanalytic theory, and this not just explicitly and by reinforcement of the kind gleaned from clinical observation, but by a force of conceptual provenance. As Eugene Webb writes:

One problem with theories focused on the psychology of the unconscious is that they may reduce religious thought, aspirations, and behavior to mere epiphenomena of impersonal forces that are thought to drive religion, as it were, from behind. They may even attempt to explain religious thought and aspiration as mere 'symptoms' of an underlying psychological disorder.[51]

In spite of this perspicacious claim, we cannot lay the blame for such an explanation of religion totally on psychoanalytic theories fixed on the unconscious or personally on the "father" of these theories, Sigmund Freud. Freud's sentiments towards religion were, in actuality, anything but consistent. Indeed, on this account, "it takes a very dedicated Freudian," as Anthony Storr writes in his superb study of Freud and Freudian theory, "to accept Freud's ideas about religion."[52] As the priest-psychologist José Juan del Col says in his extensive commentary on Freud's psychoanalytic theories and religion, his views on religion were quite "ambiguous," making him neither a candidate for "exorcism" nor for "canonization" by the religious world.[53] There is no doubt whatsoever that he

50. *Ibid.*

51. Eugene Webb, "Religious Thought and the Psychology of World Views [2006]," TMs (photocopy), p. 169.

52. Anthony Storr and Anthony Stevens, *Freud and Jung: A Dual Introduction* (New York: Barnes and Noble Books, 1998), p. 127.

53. José Juan del Col, *Psicoanálisis de Freud y Religión: Estado Actual de Am-*

was the victim of anti-Semitism, as evidenced by a somewhat-furtive allusion to the issue in his *Interpretation of Dreams*.[54] Indeed, he was forced to leave Austria by the Nazis in 1938, taking refuge in London, where he died the next year. This victimization accounts in part for his often hostile statements about Christianity (which, "with respect to Judaism," he considered "a cultural regression"[55]), just as his views of the Jewish religion as a "fossil" were a self-protective reaction, perhaps, to the anti-Semitic spirit of his times. And in his famous work, *The Future of an Illusion*, he is candid in his dismissal of religious beliefs as psychological artifacts. It is perhaps from these anti-religious sentiments that a generation of psychologists, while they may have broken ranks with orthodox Freudianism, have nonetheless concluded, with the "anti-religious" Freud, that emotional health of religious origin is an oxymoron. In the words of Albert Ellis, "Religiosity . . . is equivalent to irrational thinking and emotional disturbance."[56] The so-called "mainline" Neo-Freudians, such as Alfred Adler or Karen Horney (whose work had some influence on the thinking of Ellis), though perhaps less strident in their break with his psychoanalytic theories, are thought to fall in line, to one degree or another, with Freud's misgivings about religion.[57]

---

bigüedades por Resolver (Freudian psychoanalysis and religion: The present state of ambiguities to be resolved) (Bahía Blanca and Buenos Aires: Instituto Superior "Juan XXIII" and Centro Salesiano de Estudios "San Juan Bosco," 1996), p. 249.

54. Sigmund Freud, *Interpretation of Dreams* (Harmondsworth, England: Pelican Books, 1976), p. 304.

55. Col, *Psicoanálisis de Freud*, p. 121.

56. Quoted in Susan Larson, "Forgotten Factor," p. 84.

57. The shades of anti-religious sentiments among Freudian dissenters are subtle, ranging from a stark rejection of religion to a kind of mildly anti-religious neutrality, of which Erich Fromm is a typical example. Concerning the origin of belief in God, Fromm was of the opinion that God was an ideal of the self-actualized human and thus, of course, the product of humanistic ideals. (See Mario Aletti, *Psicologia, Psicoanalisi, e Religione* [Psychology, psychoanalysis, and religion] [Bologna: Edizioni Dehoniana Bologna, 1992], p. 52.) About the interaction between science and faith, in a response to the question of whether the psychoanalyst and priest "are . . . allies who work for the same ends and who should supplement and interpenetrate each other's field," Fromm asserted that "to set up alternatives of either irreconcilable opposition *or* identity of interest is fallacious" (emphasis mine). He sees "the relationship between religion and psychoanalysis" as "too complex to be forced into either one of these simple and convenient attitudes" (Erich Fromm, *Psychoanalysis and Religion* [London: Victor Gollancz Ltd., 1951], pp. 15-16). I should note that Karen Horney, despite Fromm's acknowledgment of her influence on his work in general, and her alleged hostility to religion aside, seems, in fact, to have had more than a feeling of anti-religious neutrality towards religion later in her life.

In contrast to this hostile attitude towards religion perpetuated by psycho-analysis, when the opportunity arose to lament over the pejorative effect of his atheistic views on his religious colleagues, its founder did so with what appears to be sincere agony and marked misgivings. Thus, in a letter to his friend, the Lutheran clergyman and psychoanalyst Oskar Pfister,[58] following the publication of *The Future of an Illusion,* he wrote: "I . . . fear . . . that such a public profession of my attitude will be painful to you."[59] In yet another place, Freud assured Pfister that, "[I]n matters of ethics, religion, and philosophy there remain differences between us which neither you nor I regard as a gulf."[60] There is not even a hint of hostility towards this Lutheran clergyman, with whom Freud frequently corresponded.[61] If his atheism was militant, it was certainly contracted, in that militancy, by his friendship and collaboration with colleagues holding overtly religious views—colleagues whom he respected and certainly never characterized as suffering from psychological pathology on account of their religiosity. Hence, Pfister's response to the foregoing statement by Freud: "You

---

"Over the passage of time," a student of her religious beliefs recently wrote, "Horney considered herself a part of the plan of God for the salvation of mankind" (Georgios Barbatsoulias, *He Neurose Kata ten Karen Horney kai Hoi Anthropologikes Theoreseis tou Hag. Maximou tou Homologetou: Synkritike Melete* [Neurosis according to Karen Horney and the anthropological aspects (perspectives) of St. Maximos the Confessor: A comparative study] [Athens: Ekdoseis Akritas, 2004], p. 50). This observation notwithstanding, Horney's childhood experiences with rigid religious discipline that she associated with a stern, unloving father created in her an implacable resentment of religion that in part led to her endorsement of Freud's views about religion, and which diminished only slowly.

58. For a brief but insightful observations about Pfister's outlook on theology and psychotherapy, see Kurt Lüthi and Koloman N. Micskey (Hgg. [eds.]), *Theologie in Dialog Mit Freud und Seiner Wirkungsgeschichte* (Theology in dialogue with Freud and the history of his impact) (Vienna, Cologne, and Weimar: Bühlau Verlag, 1991), pp. 11-13.

59. *Psychoanalysis and Faith: the Letters of Sigmund Freud & Oskar Pfister,* trans. Eric Mosbacher and ed. H. Meng and E.L. Freud (New York: Basic Books, 1963), p. 110.

60. *Ibid.,* p. 85.

61. The Spanish theologian and psychologist Ricardo Cabezas de Herrera Fernández, in his *Freud: El Teólogo Negativo* (Freud, the negative theologian) (Salamanca: Universidad Pontificia de Salamanca, 1989), has remarked that Freud's connection with religion was always in the context of its pathological expression in patients whom he treated. Pfister was Freud's sole contact with a healthy believer and, as Dr. Cabezas de Herrera says, prompted Freud to admit that the clergyman-psychologist was a "contradiction" to his "prejudices" about religion (p. 63).

have always been tolerant towards me."[62] It is also the case that Freud's occasional tolerance of religion stems from the fact that his "portrayal of the human condition," as the American religious writer Kenneth Boa has remarked, "yields significant points of correlation with the Christian understanding of sin, guilt, and the need for redemption."[63] It is very important that we emphasize these points of correlation, since they go beyond Christianity to religion in general, where human peccability, guilt, and restoration are universal themes. They bring us to an understanding of how Freud found himself—even within the confines of what he saw as his rigidly defined psychoanalytic arena—naturally sympathetic to many of the precepts of religion and their counterparts in psychological preoccupations and attributes that Freud considered universal to the human predicament. This less inimical attitude of his also has its legacy in modern psychology, even if it has not been the dominant one.

In addressing those voices in psychoanalysis that have been more sympathetic to religion, we cannot, of course, ignore Carl Jung, whose filial ties with Freudian psychoanalysis were eventually severed at every level: personally, conceptually, and clinically, and most notably in his attitude towards the importance of religion in human psychology. Thomas Szasz writes that

> [t]hroughout his long life, Jung . . . struggled with the dilemma of whether to classify psychotherapy as medical or a religious enterprise. . . . [O]n the whole, he assumed a more consistently antimedical and proreligious position on it than did Freud. . . . In fact, the break between Freud and Jung, usually thought to center on their disagreement about the significance of sexuality in the etiology and therapy of the neuroses, lies much deeper.[64]

In embracing the importance of religion, Jung was not so much concerned with "belief" in God, as Andrew Fuller asserts, but with *knowledge* of God. God, he says, was for Jung "the most immediate and certain experience of all," since he believed that "no one would talk of God if God were not a psychological fact of immediate experience."[65] Oddly enough, Jung, perhaps because of the dominant

---

62. *Ibid.*, p. 110.

63. Kenneth Boa, *Augustine to Freud: What Theologians and Psychologists Tell Us About Human Nature (And Why It Matters)* (Nashville: Broadman and Holman Publishers, 2004), p. 141.

64. Thomas Szasz, "Psychotherapy: Medicine, Religion, and Power," in *Philosophy, Religion, and Psychotherapy: Essays in the Philosophical Foundations of Psychotherapy,* ed. Paul W. Sharkey (Washington, DC: University Press of America, 1982), p. 144.

65. Andrew Reid Fuller, *Psychology and Religion: Eight Points of View* (Washington, DC: University Press of America, 1986), p. 78.

anti-religious ethos in psychotherapy, protested against those who characterized him as religious. He considered himself an "empirical scientist." However, "Jung's protestations notwithstanding," as Jungian analyst Lawrence Jaffe argues, "his psychology can be considered a kind of religion; . . . a new kind of religion—a religion of experience."[66] As one pastoral counselor has opined, "[i]n both Jewish and Christian theology, the starting point for understanding what it is to be human is the affirmation that human beings are created in the image of God." In precisely this spirit, he continues, Jung "asserts that the archetype of the self is indistinguishable from the image of God (God-image) conceived of by early Christian thinkers as the likeness of God imprinted in the human soul at creation."[67] Jung presents us, in short, with a "more elevated conception of man than that of Freud."[68] We also see this same objectivity towards religion in Karl Jaspers, who, in discarding Freudian orthodoxy, also discarded Freud's sometimes-myopic religious view. Thus, Jaspers dismisses the idea that religion and psychopathology are necessarily connected, stating that "[t]he statistical investigation of various faiths has given us the fact that the largest numbers of disorders are to be found among *the fringe supporters* of various sects."[69] Likewise, the French psychoanalyst Jacques Lacan openly challenged Freud's view of religion, taking on what he saw as Freud's misapprehensions about religion and psychology in the same way that, in the words of one author, "the Fathers of the Church" held forth against "heresies in religion."[70] This is not to say that Lacan is, as some—in my opinion, wrongly—think, an apologist for traditional theology, except perhaps as it transcends the idea that theology is "defined by the object of its inquiry,"[71] hence rendering Lacan's theological discourse theologi-

---

66. Lawrence W. Jaffe, *Liberating the Heart: Spirituality and Jungian Psychology* (Toronto: Inner City Books, 1990), p. 19.

67. Fuller, *Psychology and Religion,* p. 78.

68. Juan Bautista Torelló, *Psicoanálisis y Confesión* (Psychoanalysis and confession), trans. José Luis Martín, 2nd edition, revised (Madrid: Ediciones Rialp, S.A., 1974), p. 92. Dr. Thomas Brecht, a Jungian clinical psychologist, and I have touched on the subject of Eastern Christian theology and anthropology and Jung's views about God and man in our essay, "Jung and the Mystical Theology of the Eastern Orthodox Church: Comments on Common Ground," *Pastoral Psychology*, Vol. 37, no. 4 (1990), esp. pp. 100-102.

69. Karl Jaspers, *General Psychopathology,* trans. J. Hoenig and Marian W. Hamilton (Baltimore and London: The Johns Hopkins University Press, 1997), Vol. 1, pp. 723-724.

70. Sofia Chraïbi, *Jacques Lacan: Docteur de l'Église au Service de la Psychoanalyse* (Jacques Lacan: Doctor of the church in the service of psychoanalysis) (Paris: François Xavier de Guibert, 2000), p. 78.

71. This point is made by Charles E. Winquist in his interesting essay "Lacan and

cally avant-garde, if not exotic. It is to say, however, that he is a vivid example, along with Jung and Jaspers, of significant figures in the history of psychoanalysis who broke with Freud's thoughts about religion.

Freud and psychoanalysis, it seems to me, are not ultimately responsible for the hostility towards religion that so marked the development of contemporary psychology—whatever Freud or the various psychoanalytical schools that derived from his theories may have thought about the source or content of religious beliefs or the nature of religious practice and observance. Rather, this oppugnancy originates in the endeavor to explain and describe religious phenomena from a psychoanalytical standpoint: from the standpoint of a discipline, as Karl Jaspers once admitted, that has *"keine systematische Grundlage"*;[72] that is, which lacks a foundational system that can guide it in dealing with what lies beyond its phenomenological purview. If, as Professor Webb suggests, theories rising out of psychologies focused on the unconscious tend to attribute religious phenomena to pathological psychological processes, the mental health sciences and religion are actually separated *only* at the conceptual level; that is, at the point where religious phenomena become one with pathology—with delusion, psychoses, and severe mental disorders. But causality, once this connection is established, takes on an *a priori* status: either mental illness lies at the root of religion or religion at that of mental illness. This conundrum, in which religion can do no good, is also intimately related to the enduring tension which Freud posited between psychoanalysis and religion, a kind of self-fulfilling conceptual *axiom* that forever separated the two fields: "religion was 'the other' on which psychoanalysis works out its own self-definition, the means by which it discovers its own historical uniqueness, the meaning of its own destiny."[73] As Peter Homans has described this axiom in function, "Psychology has arisen in direct proportion to the decline of the power of religion."[74] The separation of psychoanalysis from

---

Theological Discourse," chapter 1 in *Lacan and Theological Discourse,* ed. Edith Wyschogrod, David Crownfield, and Karl Raschke (Albany, NY: State University of New York Press, 1989), p. 30.

72. Dr. Karl Jaspers, *Allgemeine Psychopathologie: Ein Leitfaden für Studierende, Ärzte, und Psychologen* (General psychopathology: A guide for students, physicians, and psychologists) (Berlin: Verlag von Julius Springer, 1913), p. 12.

73. Peter Homans, Introduction to *Childhood and Selfhood: Essays on Tradition, Religion, and Modernity in the Psychology of Erik H. Erikson,* ed. Peter Homans (Lewisburg: Bucknell University Press; London: Associated University Presses, 1978), p. 31.

74. Quoted by Frederika R. Halligan and John J. Shea in the Introduction to *The Fires of Desire: Erotic Energies and the Spiritual Quest,* ed. Frederika R. Halligan and John J. Shea (New York: The Crossroad Publishing Company, 1992), p. 13.

religion became, for Freud, in many ways a *sine qua non* for the integrity of the psychoanalytic process; in opposition to religion, that process came into its own. Many mental health care professionals have, without realizing it, taken on this Freudian conceptual struggle without a full awareness of what they are doing, thereby clouding their objective view of the role of religion in mental health.

Returning to the antipathetic spirit of psychology and psychiatry which the authors of the *Handbook of Religion and Health* encountered and confronted in their research, one very important area of study—the role of religion in schizophrenia—stands out as a salient example of how this spirit has often vitiated clinical studies and led to unfounded conclusions about the negative role of religion in mental health. It has, of course, long been observed in the literature and claimed in clinical statistics that schizophrenic patients exhibit an inordinate interest in religious issues and employ religious language and images in describing their delusions and hallucinations, which have correspondingly significant religious content. This has simply served to reinforce, for many years, prejudices based on insufficient and misleading data. Let us look, for example, at the long-held idea that religious conversion of a dramatic type, as opposed to conversion in a slow process of reflection and spiritual searching, is somehow closely connected to schizophrenic decomposition, and especially when dramatic conversion occurs in young adulthood. In fact, as the authors of the *Handbook of Religion and Health* determined by carefully reviewing the literature, there emerged some evidence that "schizophrenics were *less* likely than normal persons to have religious conversion experiences."[75] Similarly, they examined a number of studies that purported to have found an increased occurrence of schizophrenics "among cloistered, exclusively contemplative nuns."[76] After scrutinizing these studies, they concluded that there were serious flaws in them. They cite evidence from far more careful and controlled studies that indicate there is actually either a slightly lower incidence of schizophrenia among women religious than the general female population or no difference at all. In general, they conclude that there is no established link between religiosity and schizophrenia, a finding consistent with their findings regarding the nexus between religion and mental illness in general:

> [T]he evidence linking religiousness and schizotypal thinking, psychoticism, psychosis, or schizophrenia is inconsistent. All of the studies reviewed provide no information about causality. Schizophrenia may be characterized by a certain type of hyperreligiosity; conversely, chronically mentally ill adults often

---

75. Koenig *et al.*, *Handbook of Religion and Health*, p. 160 (emphasis mine).
76. *Ibid.*, p. 158.

turn to religion for comfort. Finally, religious beliefs and expressions of relig-
iousness in schizophrenic and psychotic persons may be quite different from
those in normal persons.[77]

One particularly perplexing problem for mental health professionals is "demonic possession." It commonly entails a set of bizarre behaviors that most psychologists or psychiatrists have been trained to associate with schizophrenic or
psychotic states. Certain religious groups, however, argue that "evil spiritual
powers" are at the root of such behavior. They maintain that personal agency is
lost when persons are taken over by evil spirits and that the "possessed" simply
carry out the will of these spirits or demons, or become victims of the negative
effects of their presence. In Appendix I of the DSM-IV, several instances of
what are called, in the cultures in which they are found, demonic possession are
euphemistically described as "culture-bound syndromes" or "recurrent, locally-
specific patterns of aberrant behavior and troubling experience" putatively identified by the indigenous population as "'illnesses' or at least afflictions."[78] Two
salient examples of such afflictions, along with their physiological consequences
(from fitful sleep, crying, vomiting or fever, in the first instance, to trance-like
states or personality changes, in the second), are "*mal de ojo*," or the evil eye,
which is "widely found in Mediterranean cultures and elsewhere in the world,"
and spells, "a culture-specific syndrome . . . seen among African Americans and
European Americans from the southern United States." In the case of spells, the
DSM-IV acknowledges that these "are not considered to be medical events in
the folk tradition" and that they "may be misconstrued as psychotic episodes in
clinical settings."[79] This attempt to explain demonic possession in culturally
sensitive terms results in a rather equivocal and wholly unnecessary conceptual
fogginess that does little to find an operational definition of the problem. It also
fails to address the claim by the religious groups in question that schizophrenic
and psychotic symptoms can be traced to evil spirits.

    Koenig, McCullough, and Larson tackle demonic possession directly, offer-
ing basic operational definitions that lead to helpful strategies for approaching
this important issue—one that has contributed significantly to the idea that religion fosters maladaptive behaviors or confuses mental illness for supernatural
experiences. They begin with a clear definitional statement: "[S]ome Christian
fundamentalists have maintained that the bizarre behaviors of schizophrenics
and psychotic persons are due to demonic possession." They then go on to ob-

---

77. *Ibid.*, p.162.
78. *Diagnostic and Statistical Manual*, p. 844.
79. *Ibid.*, pp. 846-847.

serve that individuals who have been diagnosed as schizophrenics do not react to the religious rituals (exorcisms) that are said to treat possession; rather, "they invariably remain schizophrenic and require pharmacologic treatment for their illness."[80] This is a strong argument against a demonic cause for such behaviors. However, the authors acknowledge that a number of psychologists and psychiatrists have seriously investigated demonic possession as a phenomenon unto itself, in an attempt to differentiate it, in terms of its etiology and symptomology, from psychological disorders *per se.* They specifically mention the work of the Duke University psychiatrist William P. Wilson, who has tried to distinguish between the characteristics of demonic possession and schizophrenia and to establish them as discrete phenomena. "According to Wilson," Koenig *et al.* state, "the possessed person does not have the affective changes (blunting of affect), the disturbance of thought (looseness of association), or the ambivalence usually seen in schizophrenia."[81] They also refer to the pioneering work of the late psychiatrist M. Scott Peck, the author of a popular book that brought to the forefront the idea that demonic possession might, indeed, be something distinct from psychopathological disorders as we normally understand them. His book, *People of the Lie: The Hope for Healing Human Evil,*[82] describes his experiences with individuals claiming to be possessed, a circumstance in which there is a palpable "presence of evil," as the *Handbook of Religion and Health* states, that "does not characterize the schizophrenic state."[83]

Citing my research on demonic possession,[84] Jean-Claude Larchet, the French philosopher and Patristic scholar, draws attention to the fact that various American psychiatrists, including Peck, have in fact "broken . . . with the naturalistic tradition," which dismisses the phenomenon of demonic possession as delusional, and have approached both possession and the content of the experiences reported by allegedly possessed individuals "as though they were genuine" and as if "they corresponded to an objective reality."[85] As I have further written, in

---

80. *Ibid.,* pp. 161-162.

81. *Ibid.,* p. 163. See William P. Wilson, "Religion and the Psychoses," chapter 11 in *Religion and Mental Health,* p. 166.

82. M. Scott Peck, *People of the Lie: The Hope for Healing Human Evil* (New York: Simon & Schuster, 1983).

83. Koenig *et al., Handbook of Religion and Health,* p. 163.

84. Bishop [Archbishop] Chrysostomos, "Demonology in the Orthodox Church," *The Greek Orthodox Theological Review,* Vol. 33, no. 1 (1988), pp. 55-57 *pass.*

85. Jean-Claude Larchet, *Thérapeutique des Maladies Mentales: L'Expérience de l'Orient Chrétien des Premiers Siècles* (The treatment of mental disorders: The experiences of the Christian East in the early centuries) (Paris: Les Éditions du Cerf, 1992), pp.

this respect,

> [a] number of psychologists and psychiatrists (Rogers, Maslow, Frankl) have suggested that abstract psychological needs, such as the need for love and meaning, play a powerful role in the human psyche. They have suggested that these positive abstractions have a force and impact of their own, and that they can, indeed, interact with the individual patient or therapist to effect changes in behavior. In effect, they take on a personal manifestation. One need make only a small step from this point to posit the existence of positive spiritual beings, angels in the classical Christian lexicon, that may interact with human beings at a para- or supra-psychological level. And if one can so speculate about positive spiritual forces, it follows that the same may apply to negative ones.[86]

Even those who would argue against "processes that diminish ego control," and who attribute to "unconscious structures and repressed instincts" the "pathological experience" of religious delusions such as possession, readily admit that "communion with God that reactivates archaic symbiotic structures has an ability to make a person feel secure enough to confront, and eventually resolve, unresolved conflicts" that give rise to "religious experience."[87] That is, accepting the real content of presumably delusional religious experiences can involve a process of restoration and perhaps lead to the re-establishment of cognitive self-control. From a purely practical standpoint, such acceptance empowers the patient's "worldview." As Samuel Thielman argues, even when that worldview "diverges significantly from the ever-narrowing 'mainstream' worldview of secular culture," factoring it into therapeutic protocols "is particularly important."[88]

In spite of these more enlightened attempts to deal with possession, it is still true that the mere discussion of the topic by mental health professionals almost always provokes a head-on confrontation between religion and science, since most scientists—like the majority of mental health professionals—continue to consider the phenomenon to be at the fringes of religious practice and more often than not scoff at it as an absurdity. In any event, aside from the relatively recent research to which I have referred, only a handful of people have ever

---

17-18.

86. Chrysostomos, "Demonology in the Orthodox Church," pp. 54-55.

87. Kevin Fauteux, *The Recovery of Self: Regression and Redemption in Religious Experience* (New York and Mahwah, NJ: Paulist Press, 1994), p. 4.

88. Samuel B. Thielman, M.D., Ph.D., "World View in Global Perspective," chapter 11 in *Handbook of Spirituality and Worldview in Clinical Practice,* ed. Allan M. Josephson, M.D., and John R. Peteet, M.D. (Washington, DC and London: American Psychiatric Publishing, Inc., 2004), p. 166.

thought of it as something worthy of scientific scrutiny. Among these, oddly enough, was Sigmund Freud. While Freud dismissed the idea of demons exercising agency by virtue of some power external to the human being, he did believe that there were negative dynamic forces arising from within the human psyche. Thus, though "Freud did not accept the supernatural reality" of the Devil, "we can imagine" that "at times" his "sense of possession became quite strong."[89] This notion of possession by something from within the unconscious, inner world of the person was shared by Jung, who viewed psychosis "as a state of possession, in which a highly charged unconscious content . . . overwhelmed the ego and took charge."[90] It seems to me that it is ultimately at this level—setting aside the broader question of the origin of psychological evil and avoiding, at least initially, the question of human agency in what some religious believers hold to be a spiritual, instead of psychological, disorder—that we can come to a general statement about possession that brings religion and psychoanalytic theory, at least, into agreement. Let us look, for example, at the witness of the holy men and women of the Christian desert. One of the great adepts of this laboratory of spiritual life and the quest for enlightenment, St. Sisoes (d. *ca.* 429) made the following remarkable statement to a neophyte seeker who asked him about demonic possession:

> 'What am I to do, Abba, since passions and demons beset me?' a young
> monk asked the holy Sisoes.
> 'Do not say that you are bothered by demons, child,' answered the elder,
> 'because the greater part of us are beset by our own evil desires.'[91]

Herein we bring Freudian and Jungian thought about inner evil and those things which torment the human psyche to focus on what the preeminently religious (spiritual) Abbas and Ammas (Fathers and Mothers) of the monastic desert also saw as something rising out of the unconscious, inner life of humankind. Working within that focus, we have a way to address the vexing problem of possession in its reality, reconciling both the religious and the scientific worldview—

---

89. David Bakan, "Freud's Paper on Demonological Possession," chapter 9 in *Freud and Freudians on Religion: A Reader,* ed. Donald Capps (New Haven, CT, and London: Yale University Press, 2001), p. 91.

90. Murray Stein, "From Freud to Jung and Beyond: Turning Points in Psychoanalytic and Religious Thought," chapter 1 in *The Fires of Desire*, p. 34.

91. Archimandrite [Archbishop] Chrysostomos, *The Ancient Fathers of the Desert: Translated Narratives from the* Evergetinos *on Passions and Perfection in Christ* (Brookline, MA: Hellenic College Press, 1980), p. 20.

and this without insensitivity to either.

Hope, Comfort, and Coping: the Role of Religious Belief in Mental Health

What emerges from the systematic research and careful study of the relationship between health and religion undertaken by Koenig, McCullough, and Larson is evidence that religious belief and religious practice are important factors in how people cope with illness: "When patients themselves are asked how they cope with physical health problems and other major life stressors, they frequently mention religious beliefs and practices."[92] Religion also seems to be a

---

92. Koenig *et al., Handbook of Religion and Health,* p. 94. The emphasis which Dr. Koenig and his colleagues place on the importance of measuring the effects of religion and religious practice on health by the criteria of religious coping and hope is of immense importance to a proper understanding of the positive relationship between prayer and health. For example, a recent study of 1,800 heart-bypass patients—"funded primarily by the John Templeton foundation" and widely touted in the popular media as the "largest, best-designed" study of its kind—found that subjects who were the focus of "'distant' or 'intercessory prayer'" derived no benefits from it; in fact, "patients who knew they were" being prayed for "fared worse." Studies of this kind are, despite the hyperbolic language used in the press to describe them, fraught with design flaws and conceptual limitations. In this particular study, the primary criterion for the beneficial effect of prayer was a diminution in the frequency of surgical complications ("the most common" of which "was an irregular heartbeat"). Assuming a direct and almost "magical" connection between well-being and prayer suggests some sort of sortilege; therefore, failure to verify that nexus says little of the actual and "understandable mechanisms" by which "religious faith influences people's health and well-being," as Koenig has remarked, in commenting on the study in question. Among these mechanisms, once more, are coping, hope, and comfort, among others, which were not the focus of this study and which, at any rate, cannot be approached by statistical evaluations. One is thus led to miss completely the genuine nature of the relationship between prayer and health. (See Rob Stein, "Prayer Doesn't Aid Recovery, Study Finds," *The Washington Post,* March 3, 2006, p. AO6.) It is also worthy of note that a significant body of literature associates heart disease (such as angina) and cardiac surgery (bypass surgery, heart transplantation, etc.) with depression. This makes patients suffering from heart disease especially poor experimental subjects, if for no other reason than the potential skewing of self-reported data about one's well-being or state of mind. (For further reading on this phenomenon, see an interesting monograph by Archimandrite Akakios, *The Orthodox Christian and the Boundaries of Contemporary Medical Technology* [Etna, CA: Center for Traditionalist Orthodox Studies, 1996], pp. 16-25 *pass.*)

significant source of comfort and hope to those suffering from mental disorders. Our authors make the following statement about the specific relationship between religion and schizophrenia and psychoses, with specific reference to their own religious traditions:

> In our opinion, the primary influence of Judeo-Christian beliefs and practices on schizophrenia and other psychotic disorders is in providing comfort, hope, and a supportive community to individuals who must cope with their emotionally devastating, largely biological illnesses.[93]

Applying this opinion more generally, they conclude that

> religion provides a powerful source of comfort and hope for many persons with chronic mental illness. Religious or spiritual interventions may help these persons utilize their spiritual resources to improve functioning, reduce isolation, and facilitate healing.[94]

To place this point in what is perhaps a more overtly religious context and to shift the agency in coping with mental illness to a spiritual force, while yet preserving intact the scientific conclusions drawn by Koenig and his colleagues, let me quote the compelling and eloquent words of the Jesuit physician, William Meissner:

> The motivating capacity of grace can intervene to shore up the self's impaired capacity and renew those basic sources of trust in and through faith. Thus, grace and faith, through the renovation and functioning of basic psychic capacities, touch every stratum of the mind and affect the functioning of all parts of the psychic organization. The psychological impact of the action of grace is profound and psychologically enriching, potentially changing, transforming, and in some sense reintegrating psyche [sic] capacities.[95]

Practical Strategies for Bringing Religion and Mental Health Concerns into Alliance

---

93. *Ibid.*, p. 163.

94. *Ibid.*, p. 165.

95. William W. Meissner, S.J., M.D., "So help me God! Do I help God or does God help me?" chapter 4 in *Does God help? Developmental and Clinical Aspects of Religious Belief,* ed. Salman Akhtar, M.D., and Henri Parens, M.D. (Northvale, NJ, and London: Jason Aronson, Inc., 2001), p. 109.

One of the more important contributions of the "Duke Doctors" and others in reinforcing an understanding of the positive effects of religious practice and belief on physical and mental health has been the development of educational and training strategies for teaching health professionals to attend to the religious concerns of their patients and for bringing clergy and clinicians together in treating the whole person, body, mind, and soul. Physicians David Larson and Francis Lu, together with science writer James Swyers, are responsible for pioneering work in this area. Worthy of particular note is their project report on religion and spirituality in the clinical setting, compiled under a grant from the Templeton Foundation.[96] They set out, in this report, evidence for the "positive relationships" between religious practice and mental illness;[97] assert that psychiatric residents in medical schools "should demonstrate competence in analyzing and discussing critically where religion/spirituality and psychiatry have overlapping (as well as opposing) concerns";[98] and develop an extensive curriculum for training mental health professional to address the religious and spiritual concerns of their patients in a systematic and comprehensive manner.

Continuing this work, Elizabeth Bowman, in her contributions to Harold Koenig's *Handbook of Religion and Mental Health,* has made very specific suggestions about just how the study of religion should be integrated into the education of mental health professionals, noting that, at the time that she was writing, "[s]cientific literature on teaching mental health trainees about religion or spirituality [was] sparse"[99]—an observation which, despite some notable progress, still generally applies today, almost a decade later. Yet, contributions like hers, expanding the foregoing project of Larson *et al.,* have helped to identify what must be done in developing seminars and courses in the relationship between religion and spirituality and mental health: what materials should be included in the curriculum, what teaching methodology should be employed, and at what point in their careers mental health professionals should be taught about religion and spirituality.[100] Psychologist Andrew Weaver, in his contribution to the same

---

96. David B. Larson, M.D., M.S.P.H., Francis G. Lu, M.D., James P. Swyers, M.A., eds., *Model Curriculum for Psychiatric Residency Training Programs: Religion and Spirituality in Clinical Practice* (Rockville, MD: National Institute for Healthcare Research, 1997).

97. *Ibid.,* p. 2.

98. *Ibid.,* p. 15.

99. Elizabeth S. Bowman, "Integrating Religion into the Education of Mental Health Professionals," chapter 25 in Koenig, *Handbook of Religion and Mental Health,* p. 367.

100. *Ibid.,* pp. 274-374 *pass.*

handbook, has put forth strong arguments for the importance of clergy in aiding "mental health specialists [to] gain access to individuals and their families in crisis who would otherwise not receive psychological care."[101] Dr. Weaver goes on to note the paucity of literature concerning "the role of clergy in mental health or in the psychological dynamics of coping."[102] He persuasively argues that more research must be done in this area, incorporating clergy into the network of mental health workers and helping them to gain training in clinical evaluation and understanding the dimensions of psychological illness and trauma.[103]

Orthodox Psychotherapy, Religion, and the Mental Health Sciences in Contemporary Greece

Without doubt, Orthodox psychotherapy, having provoked an exchange between the mental health sciences and religion, has played very much the same role in Greece that the "Duke Doctors" and their research did in bringing religion and medical science into dialogue in the United States. However, the parallels should not be overstated. Greece is a society steeped in the traditions of the Byzantine East, maintaining, even within a constitutional framework honoring the freedom of religion, a state religion, i.e., the Greek Orthodox Church. Hence, the complex interaction between religion and science in the society at large differs significantly from that of the United States. It is, of course, not our purpose to analyze the Greek social structure and the role of religion in society. However, it can be said that, while the legacy of anti-religious sentiments among mental health professionals in the United States and Great Britain (as well as much of Western Europe) has marked the development of the psychiatric and psychological sciences in Greece, too, there is the peculiar phenomenon of a strong opposition to psychiatry and psychology—and hence, psychotherapy—in the religious community. While in the West, one may find various sectarian objections to the mental health sciences, these certainly do not carry with them the weight and influence of such sentiments in a religion which has both the prestige and the power of the state at its disposal, and which enjoys at least the formal fidelity of the majority of the population, where more than 95% of the population has been baptized into the Greek Orthodox Church.

---

101. Andrew J. Weaver, "Mental Health Professionals Working With Religious Leaders," chapter 24 in Koenig, *Handbook of Religion and Mental Health*, p. 350.

102. *Ibid.*, p. 352.

103. *Ibid.*, pp. 353-359 *pass.*

Dialogues between the mental health sciences and religion in Greece face formidable challenges from two powerful social forces. On the one hand, psychiatrists and psychologists, until very recently, have worked in an anti-religious professional milieu that often entails political opposition to the state church, adding to the anti-religious legacy of their profession the supplemental force of political ideology. This situation reflects in part, even to this day, sentiments formed during the Greek Civil War (1947-1949), which pitted the rabidly anti-religious Communist insurgents against a largely religious political structure. Thus it is that, in the transformation of Greece in the last few decades from a largely religious society to one that is increasingly secular in its outlook, many health science professionals are tenaciously inimical to religion and to any significant discussion of its role in a changing society, except by way of referring to its fading significance in defining Greek identity. For example, tracing the emergence, over the past forty years, of family therapy in Greece, Professor Basilia Softas-Nall of the University of Northern Colorado, following the work of Dr. Charis Katakis (founder of the Laboratory for the Study of Human Relations, and one of Greece's most eminent students of the country's social development), speaks of Greek identity solely in terms of the "conflicting conceptual systems" that distinguish traditional Greek life from a new vision of the family.

Softas-Nall writes of Katakis that, in her quest for this new vision of the Greek family, she

> interviewed a 75-year-old shepherd living in a mountainous rural village, his 45-year-old son who lived in a nearby town, and his grandson, a 25-year-old teacher who lived in Athens. One of the questions she asked all three was 'Why do people marry and have families?' She received three different answers. . . . The old shepherd, representative of the traditional-rural form of life answered, 'This is the destination [*sic*] of man.' His son, who had experienced urban life, answered, 'People get married to have children, educate them, and make them useful members of society.' The grandson swept away what they thought in one sentence by saying, 'Marriage is neither important nor necessary, what counts is the relationship.'[104]

It is significant that this transformation of social structures in Greece, where "many couples . . . [live] . . . together and have children without getting mar-

---

104. Basilia (Lia) Softas-Nall, "Reflections on Forty Years of Family Therapy, Research, and Systematic Thinking in Greece," chapter 10 in *Global Perspectives in Family Therapy,* ed. Kit S. Ng (New York and Hove, East Sussex: Brunner-Routledge, 2003), p. 129.

ried"[105]—an assertion that would simply flabbergast the immense Greek community in the diaspora, which lives with romantic images of a traditional Greek society which is quickly disappearing, even in those few places where remnants thereof can still be found—is largely understood by Greek psychiatrists and psychologists as a change in conceptual systems or a natural evolution in the identity of the family. It is rare, in the secular circles that dominate in the world of the mental health professions in Greece, to see any attention directed at the inevitable conflicts in traditional moral values and familial images that such an assault on the religious and spiritual precepts of traditional Greek life encompasses. In fact, reference to such values is often ridiculed. Hence a letter that I received from a young Greek university student who referred me to the following passage by a pious Greek physician on motherhood, which had been read in class by one of his professors with a tone of mocking derision: "In assuming the great task of motherhood, an indispensable prerequisite is the lofty cultivation of the soul and spirit of the future mother and her ability to cultivate and kindle the love of God in her children, and to rear them in a climate of maternal affection, love, stability, and patience."[106]

On the other hand, a sometimes crude attitude prevails among religious believers about the precepts of psychiatry and psychology and psychotherapeutic traditions, reinforced, as they are, by the anti-religious legacy expressed in the traditional view of mental health professions towards religion and religious practice and, of course, by the specific realities of Greek social and political life today. One can still hear reasonably educated individuals refer to psychiatry and psychotherapy as "dark arts" and, in the unfortunate residue of anti-Semitism which survives from the last century throughout the Balkans, as the "Jewish science." This suspicion of psychotherapy is also expressed in the idea that it is a threat to the Orthodox religion and incompatible with its precepts—something, as we shall see from our investigation of the teachings and practices which underlie the Greek Orthodox spiritual life, that stems from a tragic misunderstanding of the techniques and goals of responsible psychotherapy. Indeed, to illustrate the depth of this suspicion, which has no counterpart, at least on such a scale, in Western sectarian objections to the mental health sciences, let me cite the uncompromisingly negative assessment of secular psychotherapy by a Greek physician, whose positive thoughts about *Orthodox psychotherapy* I quoted earlier. His views are drawn from his personal consultations with two well-known

---

105. *Ibid.,* p. 134.

106. Stauros I. Balogiannes, *Psychiatrike kai Poimantike Psychiatrike* (Psychiatry and pastoral psychiatry [psychology]) (Thessaloniki: Ekdoseis P. Pournara, 1986), p. 11.

spiritual adepts from Mt. Athos, Fathers Porphyrios and Paisios, on the basis of whose views he concludes that psychoanalysis and Orthodox spiritual practice are incompatible. Focusing on the classical theories of Freudian psychology, he argues that one is cured of "psychic" disease through the Mysteriological (sacramental) and ascetic life of the Orthodox Church and not "through Freudian analysis."[107] He is especially critical of the small circle of priests in contemporary Greece who are both Orthodox clergymen and psychiatrists, accusing them of placing themselves in the position of "business class priests."[108] Though perhaps a bit hyperbolic in some of his language, Dr. Adamides' otherwise articulate views are not unrepresentative of a number of religious professionals in Greece who hold the mental health sciences in anything but high esteem.

The unique and peculiar circumstances that obtain in Greece notwithstanding, the clamor produced in medical and theological circles by the debate over Orthodox psychotherapy has brought religious practice and spirituality under scientific scrutiny and has helped to overcome to a significant degree the inimical attitude of many religious Greeks towards the mental health sciences. Since the scientific community in Greece has not, to date, extensively examined and studied the positive effects of religion and religious practice on mental health *per se* in a systematic or statistical way—or to the degree that this has been done in the United States—, it would perhaps be a bit bold to say that the concept of Orthodox psychotherapy has the force of scientific study to back up its precepts. However, as theologians, the spiritual adepts of the Greek Orthodox religion, and mental health professionals come into contact by way of the attention that Orthodox psychotherapy has received, it can safely be said that psychiatrists and psychologists, and even those heretofore hostile towards religion in a global sense, have begun to examine the extant studies from abroad about the positive engagement of religion and science and have initiated serious dialogues with the religious community. And while a fully developed curriculum for studying the nexus between religion and health in university medical schools and psychology faculties is far from a fact (as is also the case in the United States, I might add), conferences and discussions directed towards that end are more popular and evident.

At the same time, and much enlightened in this process by increasingly more open-minded exchanges with the circles of priest-psychiatrists to which I referred above, more perspicacious theological critics of the mental health sciences have come to understand psychotherapy in a much broader and more ob-

---

107. Adamides, *Therapeutike ton Pateron*, p. 80.
108. *Ibid.*, p. 26.

jective context than seems to have been the case in the past. There still remains, of course, the perception, among many of the more conservative clergy, that secular psychotherapy has engaged the religious community with the intention of supplanting traditional religious observance with a new-fangled path to mental and psychic restoration. This misunderstanding is reinforced by the tendency to reduce psychotherapy to Freudianism or dream analysis, or other one-dimensional visions of psychotherapy and the psychological sciences. This is especially true, ironically enough, of those directly immersed in the spiritual exercises and life from which the principles of Orthodox psychotherapy are drawn. However, the availability of scientific data about the more general compatibility of religion and mental health, as well as the emergence of a model by which to look at Orthodox spiritual life itself as therapy, has at least helped to moderate this perception. Moreover, dialogue itself has helped to focus attention on the science that supports a positive relationship between religion and spirituality and mental health—the very science that makes Orthodox psychotherapy an important example of this relationship. Finally, of course, the popularization of Orthodox psychotherapy in the United States and Western Europe, where the science behind a positive encounter between religion and the health sciences is better known, has helped to foster greater discussion in Greece and, of course, in other Orthodox countries.

Chapter II

Eastern Orthodox Theology and the Nexus Between the Body, Soul, and Spirit

> "[I]f we understand ourselves to be organic creatures, then no part can be fully disaggregated . . . , and all elements of the self are interlocked." *Carolyn T. Brown*[109]

In the past three or four decades, philosophy, psychology, and medicine in the West have consciously embraced the idea that the body and the mind, or the body and soul, are inseparable parts of the whole human person. Holistic ideas have become part of the social discourse. Whether as a consequence of this trend or as part of whatever it is that ultimately sparked it, there is a renewed interest in spirituality, in the religions of the East (where the mind-body, or soul-body, dualism that has long reigned in Western thinking holds little sway), and in philosophies and ways of thought that address the person as a whole and aim at the restoration of that wholeness. It is, indisputably, at least partly in response to this trend that the rapprochement between religion and science—and specifically between religion and the health sciences—which we described in the previous chapter came about. However, an holistic view of the human being is nothing unique to Western intellectual thought, even if the rise of rationalism and the decline in spiritual concerns that followed the Renaissance and, more strikingly, the Enlightenment have tended to separate matters of the mind from those of the body and, most certainly, of the spirit. The Greek ancients, to whom we attribute the rudimentary elements of our Western intellectual tradition, not only consistently called for an immediate engagement between philosophy and medicine,[110] but firmly believed that the human being was made up of body and soul. This

---

109. Carolyn T. Brown, *Footprints of the Soul: Uniting Spirit with Action in the World*, in *Dreaming the American Dream: Reflections on the Inner Life and Spirit of Democracy*, ed. Mark Nepo (San Francisco: Jossey-Bass [a Wiley Imprint], 2005), p. 53.

110. Professor Constantine Cavarnos cites, for example, Plutarch's "emphatic rejection of the view that the subjects of *philosophy* (*philosophia*) and *medical science* (*iatriké*) are 'separate.'" See Constantine Cavarnos, *Plutarch's Advice on Keeping Well* (Belmont, MA: Institute for Byzantine and Modern Greek Studies, 2001), pp. 15-16.

was a fundamental feature of their world-view, shaping their anthropology and their highest social and political ideals: man the rational animal, engaged in fulfilling his physical and material needs, yet accommodating, in that effort, the lofty and more noble qualities and virtues of the soul.

As Constantine Cavarnos observes, this bipartite vision of man is one of the basic elements of the philosophy of life set forth by Pythagoras, who believed that the source of human illness was a state of disharmony between the body and the soul and that wellness lay in the "process of banishing disharmony and restoring harmony in the body and the psyche."[111] Plato, too, Cavarnos says, embraced this universal teaching of the ancients about the connection between body and soul, telling us—in positing a hierarchy in that relationship—that "in the last analysis, the condition of the body is a result of the condition of the psyche."[112] He points out that certain pathological mental conditions, in which an individual is "distraught" or "incapable of exercising reason," have, according to Plato, as their "proximate cause a bad bodily state." This state, nonetheless, derives from matters of the soul and is the result of "wrong education and a wrong mode of life."[113] In Aristotle, as well, we find clear evidence of the classical Greek belief in man as a composite of body and soul,[114] in which, as Cavarnos confirms (quoting Aristotle's *Politics*), "it is natural for the body to be governed by the soul."[115] All in all, then, in addition to believing that the human being is made up of body and soul and that the soul dominates the body, the Greek ancients also maintain that a proper and harmonious interaction between the body and soul is the source of human health and reflects a correct way of life; indeed,

---

111. Constantine Cavarnos, *Pythagoras on the Fine Arts as Therapy* (Belmont, MA: Institute for Byzantine and Modern Greek Studies, 1994), p. 24.

112. Constantine Cavarnos, *Fine Arts as Therapy: Plato's Teaching Organized and Discussed* (Belmont, MA: Institute for Byzantine and Modern Greek Studies, 1998), p. 14.

113. *Ibid.,* p. 29. At this juncture, it should also be said that there have been a few psychoanalysts who, though certainly rare exceptions, even early on in the development of the psychoanalytic movement held to a holistic view of the human being that included spiritual elements. One such example was the Venetian psychiatrist Robert Assagioli (1888-1974), a student of Freud and the father of so-called "psychosynthesis." His psychosynthetic system envisioned a "higher Self" that served to bring about harmony in the whole human being—mind, body, and spirit. See a synopsis of his ideas in *Psychosynthesis: A Manual of Principles and Techniques* (New York: Hobbs, Dorman, 1965).

114. Constantine Cavarnos, *Aristotle's Theory of the Fine Arts: With Special Reference to Their Value in Education and Therapy* (Belmont, MA: Institute for Byzantine and Modern Greek Studies, 2001), pp. 15-16.

115. *Ibid.,* p. 23.

it is the stuff of that "wonder" that is man at his best and which Sophocles so eloquently praises in his *Antigone*: "Polla ta deina kouden anthropou deinoteron pelei (Wonders are many, and none is more wonderful than man)."[116]

The Anthropology of the Greek Fathers

The Judeo-Christian tradition (if I may be allowed that somewhat imprecise and often misused designation), with its undeniable influence on the development of Western intellectual trends, also emphasizes, of course, the nexus between the body, soul, and mind, as evidenced by—if nothing else—the fact that it was the very object of the counter-trend of the rationalist tradition, which sought to separate the body from the mind and soul and, ultimately, to engender the Cartesian body-mind dualism, in its various forms, that has so long preoccupied Western philosophy. Within the Christian tradition, the writings of the Greek Fathers have always underscored the unity of body and soul with special emphasis. As Jean-Claude Larchet writes:

> [T]he Fathers strive constantly to defend a balance in understanding the constitution of the human being: the two substances which comprise him are distinct without being separated and united without being confused. 'The soul is united to the body,' St. Symeon the New Theologian writes, 'in an unutterable and indiscernible manner, in a fusion without admixture or confusion.'[117]

It is not by accident, of course, that the Patristic language which Larchet cites—nomenclature typical of that used by the Greek Fathers—is reminiscent of the language of the Christological controversies, which resulted, in the mid-fifth century, in a schism between the so-called "Chalcedonian" and "Non-Chalcedonian" Christian communities that persists to this day. The issues raised, in the attempt to describe the Nature of God, and that led to the Synod of Chalcedon (451), mirror Patristic concerns about the nature of man. While contemporary theologians often dismiss these controversies as meaningless academic arguments over "terminology" and inessentials, they were, in actuality, centered on complex, technical distinctions and refinements in language that touched on essential conceptual distinctions with immense soteriological importance. The vocabulary which the disputants used was designed to safeguard the integrity of the Christian understanding of God, the human being, and the image of God in

---

116. Sophocles, "Antigone," in *Fabulae,* ed. A.C. Pearson, reprint (Oxonii: E Typographeo Clarendoniano, 1975), ll. 332-333.

117. Larchet, *Thérapeutique des Maladies Mentales,* p. 29.

man, in the light of the Incarnation.

The reduction of such vital concerns to supposed matters of terminology is no more intelligent or historically valid than the popular pseudo-intellectual and nescient penchant for portraying the Emperor Constantine as a non-believer who, out of political motivation, *dictated* to the assembly of Church Fathers the theological formulae that they sanctioned at the Nicene Synod in 325. According to the vapid popular myth of a Christianity created by imperial machination, rather than attempting to preserve the core of vital Christian experience in which Trinitarian and Christological doctrines were reified, "Roman Orthodoxy," this phantom of a post-Nicene Christianity serving the ends of theocratic imperialism, "transformed a large portion of the Christian East into heretics."[118] This is not unlike another absurdity peddled by purveyors of pulp fiction passing as historical fact: the contention, proffered with anserine consequences, that the orthodox Canon of Scripture adopted by the early Church deliberately obfuscated the genuine Christian tradition, rather than contain it and protect it (as it candidly purported to do) from extraneous influences. The fact is that, by closely defining the nature of the human soul, as we shall see, the Greek Fathers sought to preserve an understanding of human nature that was implicit in and, as I said above, of immense importance to the unique soteriological scheme of the Christian East. By envisioning Christ as the Divine *Archetypon,* for the Orthodox believer, an imprecise definition or description of His Nature directly impinges on how one sees and grasps Christ's role in the sanctification and deification of the

---

118. See Reza Aslan, *No god but God: The Origins, Evolution, and Future of Islam* (New York: Random House, 2005), p. 11. Referring to misapprehensions like those of Aslan, and reacting to what she sees as the literalism of Isaac Newton's approach to Trinitarian doctrine, Karen Armstrong makes some insightful statements about the actual *theological* principles underlying the "Roman Orthodoxy" of Constantinople: "The Greek Orthodox theologians of the fourth century," she argues, spoke of the Trinity "precisely as *mythos*, similar to that later created by the Jewish Kabbalists. As Gregory of Nyssa had explained, the three *hypostases* of Father, Son, and Spirit were not objective facts but simply 'terms that we use' to express the way in which the 'unnameable and unspeakable' divine nature (*ousia*) adapts itself to the limitations of our human minds. It made no sense outside the cultic context of prayer, contemplation, and liturgy" (Karen Armstrong, *The Battle for God: A History of Fundamentalism* [New York: The Random House Publishing Group, 2001], p. 69). Though one may perhaps rightly entertain some reservations about her sometimes bold assumptions in the realm of comparative religion, and while the reader must be careful to understand the words "myth" and "fact" in the classical sense in which she uses them, Armstrong's focus on doctrine formed in response to religious experience ("prayer, contemplation, and liturgy") effectively leads us away from just the kind of theological and historical superficiality which I have criticized here.

human being. In becoming man, Christ "assumed a complete human nature, made up of soul and body, and it is the human in his entirety, body and soul," who is "saved and divinized," according to Orthodox soteriology.[119]

Aside from maintaining that the body and soul are united integrally and that, as Larchet observes (paraphrasing St. Maximos the Confessor [d. 662]), "every action and every movement of the human being is at once an act of his soul and of his body"[120] (a coincidence of action and movement, as St. Maximos elsewhere states, which is ideally achieved by "one who brings the body into harmony with the soul [ho harmosamenos to soma pros ten psychen]"[121]), the Greek Fathers also insist on the *exclusively* bipartite nature of man. That is, they reject the idea that the human being is comprised of three distinct elements—body, soul, and spirit (mind or intellect)—and insist that he is, as we have said, understood as a composite of body and soul alone. The tripartite concept of human composition can be found in two forms: in the rather crude and inchoate idea, so often expressed in contemporary thought, that the human being is made up of a body, a mind (or intellect), and a separate spiritual component, the soul;

---

119. Jean-Claude Larchet, *La Divinisation de l'Homme Selon Saint Maxime le Confesseur* (The divinization of man according to St. Maximos the Confessor) (Paris: Les Éditions du Cerf, 1996), pp. 640-641.

120. *Ibid.,* p. 30.

121. St. Maximos the Confessor, "Peri Theologias kai tes Ensarkou Oikonomias tou Hyiou tou Theou, Pros Thalassion" (Regarding theology and the incarnate oeconomy of the Son of God, to Thalassios), in *Philokalia ton Hieron Neptikon* (Philokalia of the sacred neptic fathers) (Athens: Ekdotikos Oikos "Aster," 1975) [hereafter, *Philokalia*], Vol. 2, p. 90. This ideal spiritual goal of "harmony," I might observe, is what St. Gregory of Nyssa (d. *ca.* 385) considers the purpose of man's creation, "by conceiving man," as the historian John Cavarnos says, "as a link between the spiritual and sensible worlds." (See John Cavarnos, *St. Gregory of Nyssa and the Human Soul: Its Nature, Origin, Relation to the Body, Faculties, and Destiny*, ed. and revised by Constantine Cavarnos [Belmont, MA: Institute for Byzantine and Modern Greek Studies, 2000], p. 23.) St. Gregory, of course, also believed in the integration of the soul and body as "man's true being" (*ibid.*), even if certain Western scholars, whom Dr. Cavarnos skillfully refutes, have attributed to his psychology (i.e., his understanding of the soul) certain Platonic elements inconsistent with Christian doctrine. In that respect, Gregory, in using Greek philosophical terms and imagery, Cavarnos contends, "gave new meaning to old concepts, . . . choosing and appropriating for himself whatever portions of . . . [the classical Greek philosophical corpus that] . . . seemed to him to possess the essential qualities of reason, beauty, and form, and assimilability into Christian teaching" (p. 18). The issue of the relationship between classical Hellenistic thought and Greek Patristic wisdom is one to which we will return in this chapter.

and at times, in the Christian East, in the teaching—officially condemned by the
Orthodox Church as heretical or inconsistent with the Patristic consensus—that
man is composed of body, soul, and a separate quality, the spirit, which is dis-
tinguishable from the soul. Those who argue in favor of this latter formulation
frequently do so on the basis of their interpretation of certain Scriptural and Patristic passages that seem to support a tripartite understanding of human composition. Professor Constantine Cavarnos, quoting the Greek theologian Zikos
Rossis (d. 1917), points out that, when properly understood, these Scriptural and
Patristic sources

> in essence express one and the same teaching. For 'spirit' does not constitute a
> *substance* distinct from the soul and hence is *not a third element of man,* but is
> a higher *power* of one and the same immaterial substance, that is, of the soul, or
> signifies the *grace* and gift of the Divine Spirit, which does not constitute an
> element of man, but only illuminates and sanctifies his soul.[122]

In like manner, one may dismiss more incondite efforts to trichotomize human
composition by observing that, for the Greek Fathers, the things of the mind or
intellect, including reason, are considered faculties of the soul, endowed with the
qualities of the soul. This is affirmed by St. Anthony the Great (d. 356), who asserts that, "[w]ith regard to the body, man is mortal, while, with regard to the
intellect (*nous*) and reason (*logos*), he is immortal."[123] Thus, when they speak of
body, soul, and spirit (or mind), Eastern Orthodox theologians inevitably do so
with clear reference to, and in the context of, the dichotomous nature of the human being.

We should also note that in Orthodox anthropology, the integral union of
the body and soul is, despite the clear concinnity of the two, marked by a *hier-*

---

122. Constantine Cavarnos, *Modern Greek Thought,* 2nd printing (Belmont, MA: Institute for Byzantine and Modern Greek Studies, 1986), pp. 63-64 (italics those of
Cavarnos). See Zikos Rossis, *Systema Dogmatikes tes Orthodoxou Katholikes Ekklesias*
(System of dogmatics of the orthodox catholic church) (Athens: 1893), pp. 397-398.
Cavarnos also observes that those who point to Scriptural references which seem to make
a distinction between the soul (*psyche*) and spirit (*pneuma*) fail to understand that the
word "spirit" is alternatively used in the New Testament "to denote life," to refer to the
soul, or "occasionally . . . to denote the highest faculty of the soul, the rational, usually
spoken of in Scripture as 'mind.'" See Constantine Cavarnos, *Immortality of the Soul*
(Belmont, MA: Institute for Byzantine and Modern Greek Studies, 1993), pp. 14-15.

123. St. Anthony the Great, "Paraineseis Peri Ethous Anthropon kai Chrestes Polite-
ias" (Exhortations regarding the character of men and the virtuous way of life), in
Philokalia, Vol. 1, p. 19.

archy of interaction, in which the soul is *superior* to the body *in that interaction.* This is because the soul is immortal and immaterial, while, in man's fallen state, the body is material and mortal. This Patristic teaching is one which popular contemporary Christian ideas of the body and soul fail to acknowledge. This is especially so in the West, where the soul is often thought of as something which exists within the human body, distinct and separate from it and unmarked by any *essential interaction* with the body. The Greek Fathers teach, instead, that the soul not only "pervades (*chorousa*)" the "entire body (*holou . . . tou somatos*)," as St. Maximos the Confessor writes, but that every member of the body responds to the presence of the soul, though it is incorporeal.[124] We should also note that, following St. Paul (1 Corinthians 15:44), the Fathers very often make a distinction between the spiritual body and the physical body, or the *soma pneumatikon* and the *soma psychikon* (this latter term, literally the "psychic body," is a special term used by St. Paul to denote the physical body and does not suggest any connection with the spirit or soul, as some wrongly think). The spiritual body is the body which the human being will have in the afterlife, after the death of the physical body, when the soul and physical body are separated. It is a "resurrected" body that is both ethereal and delicate and untouched by the materiality, disease, corruption, and mortality of the fleshly body in the present life. With regard to the immortality of the soul itself, this is testified by both Scripture and the Patristic witness. Thus Professor Constantine Cavarnos has written that "the immortality of the soul is taught in the Old and the New Testaments, in the works of the Church Fathers and other ecclesiastical writers of the Orthodox Church, and in its iconography and hymnography."[125] Of the Old and New Testamental witness he says the following: "Although in neither the Old nor in the New Testament is it asserted, in so many words, that 'the soul of man is immortal,' its immortality is implicit in many things that are said in both."[126]

As we have observed, things of the intellect and reason have the immortal qualities of the soul. Dr. Cavarnos says that these powers, too, are mentioned in Scripture:

[W]e find . . . the 'heart' (*kardia*), 'intellect' (*nous, dianoia*), 'conscience' (*syneidesis*), and 'will' (*thelema*). The activities that spring from these powers and are mentioned in Scripture are emotions, desires, dreams, cares, thoughts,

---

124. St. Maximos the Confessor, "Peri Diaphoron Aporion" (Regarding various difficult texts [Ambigua]), in J.-P. Migne, *Patrologiae Cursus Completus,* Series Graeca (Paris: 1857-1866) [hereafter, *Patrologia Graeca*], Vol. 91, col. 1100AB.

125. Cavarnos, *Immortality of the Soul,* p. 13.

126. *Ibid.,* pp. 18-19.

reasoning, understanding, faith, attention, prayer, volition, self-control, remembering, and so on.[127]

These qualities, sometimes called the "powers of the soul (*dynameis tes psyches*)," are divided into three categories: a kind of basic principle of life or *élan vital* that belongs to all created things (whether plant, animal, or human); the lower and basic psychological attributes and motivations of sensation, perception, desire, instinctual drives, etc., which humans have in common with animals; and reason (*he logike dynamis*), an attribute which pertains solely to man and which he can employ, unlike animals, to control the lower and more basic psychological attributes and motivations.[128] Cavarnos observes that the power of reason, according to the Greek Fathers,

> has two distinct aspects, the contemplative or intuitive, generally called *nous,* and discursive, most often denoted by the term *dianoia*. Reason is the highest faculty in man. It is the governor (*kybernetes*) or master (*autokrator*) of the whole man, free in its activity. It is the faculty not only of knowledge, but also of inner attention or observation and of contemplation. It can observe itself as well as what is distinct from itself. Its power of attention renders it the guardian of the whole man.[129]

Citing the teachings of St. Gregory Palamas (d. 1359), he further explains that one must distinguish "between the essence (*ousia*) of the rational faculty and its 'energy' or operation (*energeia*). The energy consists of thoughts, while the essence is the power that produces these." He goes on to say, with regard to the function of the rational faculty, that

> [t]he highest activity of the rational faculty is pure prayer. In its truly natural state, reason can intuitively apprehend higher truth. . . . It is in its natural state when it is pure, free of bad or useless thoughts and feelings.[130]

Larchet says of the *nous,* or noetic faculty, in particular, that it "represents the contemplative possibilities of man. It is fundamentally, for the Fathers, that by

---

127. *Ibid.,* p. 18.

128. These three "powers" of the soul are very clearly enumerated by St. Gregory of Nyssa in his "Peri Kataskeues Anthropou" (On the make-up of man), *Patrologia Graeca,* Vol. 44, col. 237C.

129. Constantine Cavarnos, *Byzantine Thought and Art: A Collection of Essays,* 3rd printing (Belmont, MA: Institute for Byzantine and Modern Greek Studies, 1980), p. 51.

130. *Ibid.*

which man is brought to God, directed towards Him, and united with Him. . . . [I]t is, in effect, the image of God in man." Larchet pinpoints in the *nous* the "indelible mark" of man's "true nature."[131]

The Human Condition and Eastern Orthodox Cosmology

It becomes immediately apparent from what we have said about the contrast between the mortal body and the immortal soul, as well as from Larchet's pithy portrayal of the noetic faculty as a mark of true human nature, that the Greek Fathers, in describing the constitution of man, distinguish between an ideal state and the prevailing human condition. Just as its anthropology reflects the general teaching of the Judeo-Christian tradition regarding the nexus between the body and soul, so Orthodox cosmology, in concord with mainstream Christian thought, posits that the human being, in his present state, is fallen; i.e., that men and women have sullied the image of God with which they were created and lead lives that are at odds with the Divinity with which they were originally endowed by their Creator. Following the creation story in Genesis, the Greek Fathers describe man, in the prototype of Adam and Eve,[132] as having deviated from the aim and goal for which he was originally created—as a "failed god," to

---

131. Larchet, *Thérapeutique des Maladies Mentales*, pp. 37-38.

132. The creation narrative in Genesis, according to Bishop Kallistos (Ware), while "concerned with certain *religious* truths, . . . [is] . . . not to be taken as literal history. Fifteen centuries before modern Biblical criticism, Greek Fathers were already interpreting the Creation and Paradise stories symbolically rather than literally" (Timothy Ware, *The Orthodox Church,* 2nd ed. [London and New York: Penguin Books, 1993], p. 218, note 2). The Romanian theologian, Father Eugen Pentiuc, lends support to Bishop Kallistos' view when he argues that the Hebrew word "*adam,*" as it is used in the creation narrative, "connotes 'humanity' as a totality, not a particular person or individual gender. The original *adam* was, then, a single human *collective,* an undifferentiated aggregate of the male and female individuals created by God." (See Eugen J. Pentiuc, *Jesus the Messiah in the Hebrew Bible* [New York and Mahwah, NJ: Paulist Press, 2006], p. 1 [emphasis mine].) These observations argue persuasively for a non-literal or symbolic interpretation of the Genesis creation story. This is not to say, of course, that there are not Orthodox who follow a literal interpretation of the Genesis account of the creation of man. Citing a number of Patristic sources, though admittedly influenced by Protestant Evangelical commentaries on the subject, as well, a recent work by the late Father Seraphim Rose, *Genesis, Creation and Early Man: The Orthodox Christian Vision* (Platina, CA: St. Herman of Alaska Brotherhood, 2000), proffers just such an interpretation.

rephrase the ancient Greek vision of man as a "fallen god" *in illo tempore,* or some past age. It is to "missing the mark," or having taken a path of folly in the place of the road set out by the Creator, that they refer when they speak of human sin or sinfulness. (One can see both the Hebrew and Greek roots of this idea of sin in Proverbs 14:21. In the Greek *Septuaginta,* we read: "He that dishonors the needy [*penetas*] sins [*hamartanei*]."[133] The King James Version[134] of the Hebrew text of the same passage says that one "sins [*chata*]" thus, not against the needy, but against one's "neighbour [*rea*]." In the two readings, despite the variation in wording between "*penetas*" and "*rea,*" both the Greek "*hamartanei*" and the Hebrew "*chata*" derive from roots that denote a missing of the mark or target: *sin as a deviation from some aim or standard.*) The original *Lapsus,* or universal Fall of man from the Divine image and from pre-lapsarian Paradise through sin, had universal consequences, according to the Greek Fathers, for all human beings, who, though they do not share in the guilt of Adam and Eve, suffer from the consequences of the Fall. This suffering is beautifully expressed in several verses from the First Canticle of the Great Canon of St. Andrew of Crete, which is recited in Thursday Matins of the fifth week of the Orthodox Great Lent (the fast before the Feast of Pascha[135]):

> I have rivaled in transgression Adam the first-formed man, and I have found myself stripped naked of God, of the eternal kingdom and its joy, because of my sins.
>
> Woe to thee, miserable soul! How like thou art to the first Eve! For thou hast looked in wickedness and wast grievously wounded; thou hast touched the tree and rashly tasted the deceptive food.
>
> Instead of the visible Eve, I have the Eve of the mind: the passionate thought in my flesh, shewing me what seems sweet; yet whenever I taste from it, I find it bitter.

---

133. *The Septuagint with Apocrypha: Greek and English,* trans. Sir Lancelot C.L. Brenton, 3rd printing (Peabody, MA: Hendrickson Publishers, 1990), p. 801.

134. *The Holy Bible: Containing the Old and New Testaments, Translated Out of the Original Tongues and With the Former Translations Diligently Compared and Revised (Authorized King James Version)* (New York: World Publishing, n.d.), p. 530.

135. The proper term for the Orthodox Feast of the Resurrection of Christ, commonly called "Easter" in Western Christendom. "Pascha" is the Greek word for "Passover," and the Orthodox Church celebrates the Resurrection as a Christian Passover: "*Pascha Kyriou,*" or the "Passover of the Lord." The Orthodox Church still celebrates Pascha according to the fourth-century formula appointed by the First Oecumenical Synod in Nicea (i.e., on the first Sunday after the first full moon following the Vernal Equinox, and after the Jewish Passover), whereas Western Christians no longer follow this ancient dictum.

Adam was justly banished from Eden because he disobeyed one commandment of Thee, O Saviour. What then shall I suffer, for I am always reject-
ing Thy words of life?

By my own free choice I have incurred the guilt of Cain's murder. I have
killed my conscience, bringing the flesh to life and making war upon the soul
by my wicked actions.[136]

Not only has all of mankind in some way been implicated in the degradation
of humanity, in the Greek Patristic view, but as a result of the besmirching of the
image of God in man, and as a consequence of this tragic change in the course
of the human being's God-ordained spiritual and ontological evolution, the essence of life itself has been distorted. St. Gregory Palamas, in a homily on this
subject, tells us that all of our "illnesses, infirmities, and other misfortunes," as
well as "death," come "from our ancestral sin in Paradise (apo tes en to parade-
iso . . . progonikes hemon hamartias)"; i.e., from the original disobedience of
our Forebears, Adam and Eve, which resulted in our exile into a "corruptible
world (*epikeron touton kosmon*)," to a "path" set by man's sin, resulting ultimately in the "final stop (*ho teleutaios stathmos*)": death. This errant course, St.
Gregory points out, was not one willed by God; rather, it was one which He
tried to impede by establishing a commandment that, should it be transgressed,
would lead to death, thus assuring human beings the freedom to prevent their
own destruction through obedience. However, the same freedom of will that
provided for man's progress in the Divine path established by God also allowed
him to choose the path of disobedience; and in deliberately abandoning God and
His "life-giving counsel (*zoopoion symboulen*)," humankind suffered tragic
consequences.

The first of these consequences, according to Palamas, was the spiritual
death of the soul: separated from God, the soul is now, "as Paul says [I St.
Timothy 5:6], dead yet still alive (*zosa tethneke*)," and "its life worse than death
(thanatou cheiron autes he zoe)," having been moved away from the good and
finding itself driven by "self-reviling evil (*autophthono kakia*)." Thereupon, St.
Gregory says, there followed the death of the body. These consequences did not
come from God, he avers, but "by reason of divine abandonment, which is precisely what sin is (ek tou aitiou tes theias enkataleipseos, hoper estin he hamar-
tia)"; they follow on man's estrangement from God and the mark or target set
for the human being by Him.[137] In falling to disobedience, man imitated the dis-

---

136. *The Lenten Triodion,* trans. Mother Mary and Archimandite Kallistos Ware (London and Boston: Faber and Faber, 1978), pp. 378-379.

137. St. Gregory Palamas, "Homilia XXXI: Ekphonetheisa en Lite Teloumene Kata

obedience of Satan, "the spiritual serpent and source of evil (*ho archekakos ophis*)," who first separated from God and who, St. Gregory tells us, is not dead, since death has "no essence," except through "the casting-off of true life (*apobolen ontos zoes*)." Bringing man to "partake in his own death (pros koinonian tes oikeias nekroseos tou)," Satan, "making himself a death-bestowing spirit (nekropoion heauton poiei pneuma),"[138] ushered in, beyond the tragedy of spiritual death, man's fall to illness and, again, physical death. Thus, in the words of St. Gregory of Nyssa, man's Fall clothed him in the "flesh" (St. Gregory Palamas, following Gregory of Nyssa, remarks that lapsed humans assumed "coats of skin [*dermatinous chitonas*]"[139]), introducing him to sexuality, conception, birth, irrationality, and all of the debilities, foibles, and ills of fallen human nature.[140]

The Greek theologian Panayiotis Nellas writes that, because of the Fall, "the disruption which sin created in man brought with it the disruption of the cosmos." Since

> [i]n creating man in the image of the King of the ages, God made him, according to Nikitas Stithatos,[141] 'king of creation' and enabled him 'to possess within himself the inward essences, the natures and the knowledges of all things.' It was therefore unavoidable that the disruption of man should have brought about the disruption of the 'essences' and the 'natures' of beings, that is, the disruption also of creation.[142]

Father John Romanides also emphasizes, in his study of sin in the cosmology, anthropology, and soteriology of the early Greek Fathers (originally submitted,

---

ten Proten tou Augoustou" (Homily 31, delivered at the litany on the first day of August), in *Gregoriou tou Palama: Hapanta ta Erga* (Gregory Palamas: complete works), ed. Panagiotes Chrestou (Thessaloniki: Paterikai Ekdoseis "Gregorios ho Palamas," 1985) [hereafter, *Gregoriou tou Palama: Hapanta*], Vol. 10, pp. 276-282 *pass.*

138. *Ibid.,* p. 292.

139. *Ibid.,* p. 276.

140. See St. Gregory of Nyssa, "On the Making of Man," in Phillip Schaff and Henry Wace, eds., *A Select Library of the Nicene and Post-Nicene Fathers of the Christian Church,* Second Series, reprint (Grand Rapids, MI: Wm. B. Eerdmans Publishing Company, 1991) [hereafter, *Select Library*], Vol. 5, pp. 407-408 *pass.*

141. Niketas Stethatos, an eleventh-century Greek monk and theological writer (d. *ca.* 1085), was a disciple of St. Symeon the New Theologian (d. 1022).

142. Panayiotis Nellas, *Deification in Christ: Orthodox Perspectives on the Nature of the Human Person,* trans. Norman Russell (Crestwood, NY: St. Vladimir's Seminary Press, 1987), p. 85.

in 1957, as his doctoral thesis at the University of Athens[143]), the consequence of the *Lapsus* for the whole of creation: "The fall was not limited to the human race but extended to reasonless animals and reasonless nature."[144] St. Basil the Great (d. 379), in his "Peri tes tou Anthropou Kataskeues (On the make-up of man)," illustrates these devastating effects of the Fall on the whole of creation, including the animal world, by observing that the snake—the "frightful serpent (*phriktos ophis*)" of fallen nature—was once an upright creature of "affable character (*prosenes*)" and "tame (*hemeros*)."[145] In effect, the degradation of the human condition by the power of Satan is also reflected in the degradation of the cosmos by decay (illness) and deterioration (death); the Satanic bacterium of sin, which led to the abasement of the "king of creation," has infected the universe, compromising its structure and thwarting its purpose. The human being's coöperation with, and subjugation by, Satan and his powers are at the root of imperfection in all of creation:

> Despite the fact that marvelous order and harmony prevail in the cosmos, clearly demonstrating that all things are governed by God, nevertheless, there exists in it a kind of parasite that is manifested by death and consequently by disharmony in the societal relations of man. The evils that are produced by death are not from God. . . . As a result, this world which is in subjection to death and corruption cannot be considered natural, if by natural we mean the world as God intended it to be. In other words, the world is abnormal, but this

---

143. Presbyter John Sabbas Romanides, *To Propatorikon Hamartema: Etoi Symbolai eis ereunan ton proypotheseon tes didaskalias peri Propatorikou Hamartematos en te mechri tou Hag. Eirenaiou Archaia Ekklesia en antibole pros ten katholou katheuthynsin tes Orthodoxou kai tes Dytikes mechri Thoma tou Akinatou Theologias* (Ancestral sin: Namely, contributions to the study of presuppositions concerning the doctrine of ancestral sin in the ancient church to the time of St. Irenaeus vis-à-vis the general direction of Orthodox and Western theology to the time of Thomas Aquinas) (Athens: University Press, 1957).

144. John S. Romanides, *The Ancestral Sin: A Comparative Study of the Sin of Our Ancestors Adam and Eve According to the Paradigms and Doctrines of the First- and Second-Century Church and the Augustinian Formulation of Original Sin*, trans. George S. Gabriel (Ridgewood, NJ: Zephyr Publishing, 2002), p. 81. The original Greek text (see Romanides, *To Propatorikon Hamartema*, p. 72) reads, "He ptosis den perioristhe eis to anthropinon genos, alla epexetathe kai eis ten alogon physin," which might better be translated, in order to underscore the issues at hand, as follows: "The Fall was not limited to the human race but *spread* even to *dumb animals* and *inanimate nature*" (emphasis mine).

145. *Patrologia Graeca*, Vol. 30, col. 68A.

is not because of its own nature but because a parasitic force exists in it at present.

According to the later testimonies of Judaism and the earliest ones of Christianity, the devil and his demons are not only the cause of death, they are also agents of illness. . . . As created by God, the visible and invisible world is very good . . . because that is how God wanted it. This is precisely why death is the tragic outcome of man and the work of the devil.[146]

In this description of the collapse of man and the cosmos to the power of Satan by the human sin of turning from the Divine path set out for men and women by God to that trail of tribulations which, in exercising free will, men and women embraced when they succumbed to the wiles of Satan, it is essential that we understand that mankind and the world were not made victims of Divine wrath and have not been abandoned by God. Such ideas are foreign to the Greek Patristic consensus; rather, that consensus holds that human beings were infected by sin and made slaves to a demonic power which challenges and works against Divine Providence. Humankind and the world were reduced, through the Fall, to dwelling in illness and imperfection (and this, again, by man's free choice); but they were still subject to God's Grace and were not wholly separated from Him. While they were *debased* to an abnormal, unhealthy state, man and the universe were not *deprived* of the potential for perfection and a return to normality. Moreover, before the Fall, as Bishop Kallistos writes, in the teachings of the Greek Fathers, "[h]umans . . . were perfect, not so much in an actual as in a potential sense." That is, "[e]ndowed with the image [of God] from the start"—namely, as "icons" of God and His "offspring"—, "they were called to acquire the likeness [of God] by their own efforts (assisted of course by the grace of God)."[147] This striving for perfection, then, was not erased by sin; rather, in many ways it took on an even greater significance, once man had deviated from the path towards ensured perfection appointed for him by God. Not only are these points important to keep in mind, but they stand in sharp contrast to human sin and degradation as they are often understood in Western Christianity.

Bishop Kallistos further notes that

[t]his image of Adam before the fall is somewhat different from that presented by Augustine[148] and generally accepted in the west since his time. According to

---

146. Romanides, *Ancestral Sin,* pp. 82-86 *pass.*
147. Ware, *The Orthodox Church,* p. 219.
148. St. Augustine, Bishop of Hippo (d. 430).

Augustine, humans in Paradise were endowed from the start with all possible wisdom and knowledge: theirs was a realized, and in no sense potential perfection.[149]

Romanides expands on this point, contrasting the earliest theological traditions of the Greek Fathers with the theology of Augustine and later Western thinkers:

> The first theologians of the Church who dealt with the subject of the fall took the New Testament's teachings about perfection very seriously. The fall for them was not at all a juridical matter but rather the failure of man to attain to perfection and *theosis* (divinization) because he fell into the hands of him who has the power of death. Thus, salvation for them was the destruction of the power of Satan and the restoration of creation to its original destiny through the perfecting and *theosis* of man. . . . That destiny is the basis of the theology of the fall and of salvation.[150]

Sickness and death, the separation of the mortal body from the immortal soul at the time of death, and every other imperfection in man and the universe, then, are not, for the Greek Fathers, punishments brought down on man by a wrathful God;[151] they are, as the Eastern Christian tradition emphasizes, the consequences of his having missed the mark, the stuff and substance of the "ancestral curse" (the circumstance of man's "unnatural" post-lapsarian nature) that befell him

---

149. Ware, *The Orthodox Church*, p. 220.

150. Romanides, *Ancestral Sin*, p. 112.

151. Though it is not within the scope of my discussion here to develop this idea at great length, I should note that a number of the early Greek Fathers argued that the Fall of man facilitated his divinization. As Romanides summarizes this argument, drawing on the theology of Sts. Theophilos of Antioch (d. *ca.* 183-185) and Irenaeus of Lyons (d. at the end of the second or beginning of the third century), "the destiny of man was for him not to remain in the state in which God made him [*sic*] since he was made to become perfect and, thus, to be divinized. He was made needing to acquire perfection, not because he was made flawed in nature and morally deficient but because moral perfection is achieved only in total freedom" (*ibid.,* p. 126). God, respecting man's freedom, allowed him to be lured away by Satan and to fall to the illness of the ancestral curse. But the consequences of the curse were not wrathful punishments by God; rather, man's Fall through his own free will served to allow God to facilitate the human path towards divinization and perfection. This understanding—which Romanides says that Eastern Christianity holds in common with Judaism and, as we mentioned earlier, was distorted by the Augustinian tradition (*ibid.,* p. 123)—runs contrary, once more, to any idea of "original sin," the total depravation of human nature after the Fall, or some legalistic notion of man's need to justify his sin before a wrathful Creator.

through the wiles of Satan, and a departure from his true nature—from the perfection, divinization, and participation in the Divine for which he was originally created. Only by grasping these cosmological principles can one properly understand, in turn, the anthropology of the Greek Fathers and, as we shall see, the unique soteriology of the Orthodox Church and the "great divergence between the way in which the Orthodox East and Roman Catholics (as well as Protestants) see man and his relationship with God."[152]

Salvation and Restoration According to the Theological Consensus of the Greek Fathers

The teaching of the Greek Fathers on salvation cannot be understood without reference to the *apokatastasis* or "restoration" of man and the universe which it encompasses. Man is not saved, according to the soteriology of the Orthodox Church, by the mere atonement of mankind for some juridical infraction against the Will of God. Though an expiatory model of salvation can be found in some of the writings of the Greek Fathers, even in such cases, the aim of atonement is not a juridical compensation paid to God in recognition of man's sin—of reparation; rather, this model speaks of the restoration of man's oneness with God through the repentant redirection of human actions and intention, facilitated as this effort is by the loving Grace of God. This restoration captures the inclination of post-lapsarian man to return to the course set out for him by the Creator, turning from evil (which was brought about by man's deviation from God and goodness, under the influence of Satan) to the spiritual path that leads to deification[153] and the restoration of both human nature and the world to the original state of Paradise in Eden—indeed, to a state of future perfection that will, in fact, *exceed* the glory of Eden. As Vladimir Lossky describes man's pre-lapsarian state and his state after restoration, while "man was created perfect," this "does not mean that his first state is identical with his last. . . . [B]oth the cosmology and the anthropology of the Eastern Church are dynamic in charac-

---

152. Archbishop Chrysostomos, *Ortodoxia de Est si Crestinismul de Vest* (The orthodox east and the christian west), trans. Deacon Father George Balaban and Raluca Balaban (Bucharest, Romania: Editura Universitara "Ion Mincu," 2003), p. 44.

153. Or, according to St. John of Damascus (d. *ca.* 749), "participation in the Divine Radiance (metoche tes theias ellampseos)." See his "Ekdosis Akribes tes Orthodoxou Pisteos" (Exact exposition of the orthodox faith), *Patrologia Graeca,* Vol. 94, col. 924A. It is interesting to note that one finds, in this passage, an adumbration of the Essence-Energies distinction of St. Gregory Palamas (*vide infra,* Chap. 3). St. John thus contrasts "Divine Radiance," or deification, with "the Divine Essence (*ten theian ousian*)" (*ibid.*).

ter."[154]

Briefly, in presenting the idea of *apokatastasis* as a rudimentary element in the soteriology of the Eastern Fathers, I must say something about the misunderstanding of this term that can be found in many Western commentaries on the Greek Fathers and in some Orthodox writers. According to the idea of *apokatastasis*, as I said above, evil has no existence in and of itself but is, instead, a distortion or perversion of good inspired by Satanic influence. Moreover, man and the world are subject to restoration and perfection in the salvific efforts of God to free man from the ancestral curse. A clear exposition of the idea can be found in the writings of St. Gregory of Nyssa, who also argues, however, that in the restoration of all things, "there will be thanksgiving with one accord on the part of all creation," and that both the righteous and those who have been purified by the fire of Hell will find themselves in this joint act of rejoicing.[155] In so arguing, St. Gregory seems be saying that both the virtuous and those cleansed by the fires of Hell will be restored to perfection. Thus, some authorities argue that he, along with the Orthodox who honor his theological sagacity, advocated the heresies of Origen (d. 254), who was condemned by the Church for a variety of unorthodox ideas, among them the doctrine of the pre-existence of souls,[156] or the assertion that all souls—including Satan and his minions—will eventually return to God, and the teaching that Hell, or alienation from God by a rejection of His will and deliberate acts of evil without repentance, is not an eternal state.[157]

---

154. Vladimir Lossky, *The Mystical Theology of the Eastern Church,* reprinted (Crestwood, NY: St. Vladimir's Seminary Press, 1976), p. 126.

155. St. Gregory of Nyssa, "Logos Katechetikos ho Megas (Great Catechetical Discourse)" Chapter XXVI, *Patrologia Graeca,* Vol. 45, col. 69B.

156. The doctrine that the human soul exists prior to its attachment to the human body. This teaching is rejected by Orthodox Christianity on the grounds that it violates the integrity of the human being as a composite of body and soul, rendering the body inferior to the soul. Orthodox Christian doctrine, in concord with the Old Testamental record, attests that the body was created by God and that it is inherently good: "[Y]our body is the temple of the Holy Spirit, which ye have from God (hou echete apo Theou)" (I Corinthians 6:19). So it is also that, according to the teachings of the Orthodox Church, with the General Resurrection of the dead, at the end of time, the body will be resurrected and reunited to the soul.

157. As a number of Orthodox writers have pointed out, in its doctrine of *apokatastasis* the Orthodox Church has never endorsed the supposition that all human beings will eventually be saved, regardless of their spiritual state. From a psychological standpoint, alone, it is obvious that such a deterministic idea would thwart the human striving for perfection. Hence, Protopresbyter George Metallinos, Professor of Theology at the University of Athens, in his comments on the pastoral theology of St. Nicodemos the

In actuality, though he was profoundly influenced by Origen (as was his contemporary St. Gregory the Theologian [d. 389]), St. Gregory of Nyssa did not believe in the pre-existence of souls and was certainly not, as one of the first Orthodox divines to examine his writings on the restoration of man and the universe, St. Barsanouphios (d. *ca.* 540), implies (in the words of Father Florovsky), an "uncritical disciple" of Origen.[158] From a careful and critical reading of St. Gregory, one can in no way conclude that he argues against the necessity of repentance and forgiveness for the attainment of salvation; nor, to be sure, does he seem to think that everyone will ask for and receive forgiveness. Rather, he stresses that, in the face of the forgiving love of God, everyone will be given the *opportunity* to accept and follow the Will of God. Father Florovsky also points out that St. Maximos the Confessor, who undertook to study and defend the theology of St. Gregory,

> interpreted . . . [St. Gregory's] . . . doctrine of the universal restoration as the turn of every soul to the contemplation of God, which is the realization of the 'totality of the faculties of the soul.' . . . Maximus [also] distinguished between *epignosis,* the knowledge of Divine truth, and *methexis,* participation in the Di-

---

Hagiorite (d. 1809), tells us that images of the wrath of God and eternal punishment, and emphasis on acts of penitence and repentance, "more than anything else," help to maintain "the penitent in a state of constant vigilance" (Protopresbyter George Metallinos, "The *Exomologetarion* of St. Nicodemos the Hagiorite," *Orthodox Tradition,* Vol. 19, No. 1 [2002], p. 16). Father Metallinos contends that it is in an effort to make the human being "aware of the essence of sin and its devastating power" that Nicodemos and other Church Fathers employ starkly punitive imagery and language, focusing our attention on the human "capacity for Divine sonship" and perfection (p. 21). If sin (or, for that matter, spiritual struggle) had no ultimate consequence, save that of the indiscriminate restoration of all things, human action and spiritual striving would not only lack any ultimate meaning, but, as Metallinos argues, religious imagery would come to lack any motivational power.

158. [Protopresbyter] Georges Florovsky, *The Eastern Fathers of the Fourth Century,* Vol. 7 in *The Collected Works of Georges Florovsky* (Vaduz, Liechtenstein: Bücherver-triebsanstalt, 1987), p. 219. It should be noted that, despite Father Florovsky's assessment of St. Barsanouphios' comments on St. Gregory of Nyssa's views on this matter, the former nowhere suggests that the latter is a heretic. Barsanouphios concludes his considered observations with the following non-condemnatory remark: "Do not suppose that even the holy ones were able to grasp truly (*gnesios*) all of the profundities of God" (St. Barsanouphios, "Didaskalia peri ton Origenous, Evagriou, kai Didymou Phronematon [Instruction on the the opinions of Origen, Evagrios, and Didymos]," *Patrologia Graeca,* Vol. 86 [A], col. 901B).

vinity, which requires a definite movement of the will.[159]

Florovsky admits that St. Gregory does not, in fact, *clearly* make a "distinction between the consciousness of Good and the inclination of the will towards it," as does St. Maximos. But St. Maximos, in his interpretation of St. Gregory's theology, as Florovsky observes in another place, insists that "God will be everything, and in everything," but that this "deification . . . must be accepted and experienced in freedom and love."[160] Here we have a definition of *apokatastasis* which, in its carefully defined expression, confirms the orthodoxy of St. Gregory of Nyssa's doctrine of restoration and certainly contains none of the overt heresies held by Origen. We also have a lucid statement about the fundamental element of Orthodox soteriology on which I would like to build: that salvation entails the restoration of man to his pre-lapsarian state, his eventual attainment to a greater state of perfection than that which he had in the Paradise of Eden, and his deification, as the crown of Divine creation, along with the world and universe around him.

If the soteriology of the Greek Fathers rests conceptually on a restorative model of man and the world, a *sui generis* quality of that model that cannot be overstated is its Christocentricity. The entire soteriological scheme of the Orthodox Church is formed around the Person of Christ, "in Whom we all dwell and find our true identities," being, as He is, the "source" of the restored man,[161] the *novus homo,* and the source of the transformed world—a "New World" and a "New Earth"—"in which he dwells."[162] As we observed earlier, Christ represents the *Archetypon,* the Divine Archetype, of the human being as he is restored to his proper and God-ordained path to perfection and divinization (deification). Speaking of Christ as the Archetype of restored man, St. Gregory the Theologian, for example, writes in a stirring Paschal oration: "[Today] I am glorified

---

159. Florovsky, *The Eastern Fathers,* p. 219. See St. Maximos the Confessor, "Peusis, kai Apokriseis kai Eroteseis (Questions, inquiries, and responses)," No. 13, *Patrologia Graeca,* Vol. 90, col. 796A-C.

160. [Protopresbyter] Georges Florovsky, *The Byzantine Fathers of the Sixth to Eighth Century,* Vol. 9 in *The Collected Works of Georges Florovsky* (Vaduz, Liechtenstein: Büchervertriebsanstalt, 1987), p. 245.

161. Bishop [Archbishop] Chrysostomos and Reverend James Thornton, *Love,* Vol. 4 in *Themes in Orthodox Patristic Psychology* (Brookline, MA: Holy Cross Orthodox Press, 1990), p. 49.

162. Archimandrite [Archbishop] Chrysostomos, Hieromonk Auxentios, and Hierodeacon Akakios, *Contemporary Eastern Orthodox Thought: The Traditionalist Voice* (Belmont, MA: Nordland House Publishers, 1982), p. 15.

with Him . . . , today I am quickened with Him, . . . let us honor our Arche-type."[163] Similarly, St. John of Damascus, speaking of the deification of man, re-fers to the Divine image in man as it is "mingled" with Christ the "Arche-type."[164] As Metropolitan Cyprian states, Christ is the "Archetype, . . . Who will grant Grace and deification."[165] Christ the Savior and Christ the Redeemer, the focus of the Orthodox Church's ineluctably Christocentric soteriological teach-ings, also brings to those teachings a truly anthropocentric element, expressed in an intimate relationship between man and the Divine Archetype of man restored, perfected, and deified through Christ, Who, taking on human nature, perfected it, revealing, in His Person, God made man: God Incarnate, the *Theanthropos,* the God-Man, both Perfect Man (*teleios Anthropos*) *and* Perfect God (*teleios Theos*).

The idea of Christ as the restored human, the new or second Adam, taking on the flesh of man, effecting a new creation, and setting human beings once more on the path towards deification and perfection, is beautifully expressed in one of the *Theotokia* (hymns to the Virgin Mary, appointed in the *Octoechos,* the service book containing hymns for the eight modes [tones] of the weekly liturgical cycle of the Orthodox Church) for Sunday Matins in the second mode: "Most blessed art thou, O Virgin Theotokos; for through Him Who was incar-nate of thee . . . , Adam hath been restored (*anakekletai,* or, literally, 'recalled' [to new life])."[166] St. Gregory Palamas echoes this theme in the following pas-sage from one of his sermons, in which he says that the Resurrection of Christ restored Adam to immortality:

> [W]e were taken by night and seized by the shadow of death, having fallen in sin and having lost the power of seeing, which was by the Grace of God ours and with which we perceived the light that grants true life. Night and death were poured upon our nature, not because the true light withdrew, but because we turned away, no longer having within our persons an inclination towards that light which bestows life. However, . . . the Giver of eternal light and the Source of true life had mercy on us, not only coming down for our sake, be-

---

163. St. Gregory the Theologian, "First Oration: On Easter and His Reluctance," Schaff and Wace, *A Select Library,* Vol. 7, p. 203.

164. St. John of Damascus, "Homilia in Transfigurationem Domini" (Homily on the transfiguration of the Lord) *Patrologia Graeca,* Vol. 96, col. 552C.

165. Metropolitan Cyprian of Oropos and Fili, "To Archetypon Mas kai He Diaphy-laxis Apo Ta Eidola" (Our archetype and preservation from idols), *Hagios Kyprianos,* Vol. 14, no. 329 (2005), p. 235.

166. *Parakletike,* revised edition (Athens: Ekdoseis "Phos," 1987).

coming a man like us, but enduring the Cross and death for us . . . , resurrecting on the third day, showing once more that the light of eternal and immortal life in our nature was for it the light of resurrection.[167]

Vladimir Lossky draws direct lines between the image of Christ as the restored Adam and the deification of man and the universe: "Since this task of deification . . . given to man [by God] was not fulfilled by Adam, it is in the work of Christ, the second Adam, that we see what it was meant to be."[168]

Many Church Fathers, it should be noted, extend the image of Christ as the new, or second, Adam to the Virgin Mary, making the Mother of God, in this expanded imagery, a symbol of the new or second Eve in her restoration to the path towards perfection. In this way, they emphasize that the abrogation, by Christ's Incarnation and Resurrection, of the ancestral curse that fell upon Adam and Eve and their descendants is universal. Thus, St. Irenaeus of Lyons writes:

[F]or Adam had necessarily to be restored in Christ, that mortality be absorbed in immortality, and Eve in Mary, that a virgin, become the advocate of a virgin, should undo and destroy virginal disobedience by virginal obedience.[169]

St. Maximos the Confessor further clarifies this image of Eve, by asserting that the souls of those who come to resemble God through deification participate in the bodily birthgiving of the Virgin Mary in a mystical way:

Christ always desires to be born in a mystical way, becoming incarnate in those who attain salvation, and making the soul that gives birth to Him a Virgin Mother.[170]

This is an important clarification: whereas Christ, as the second Adam, *restored* humankind—men and women alike—by taking human form *as God,* the Virgin Mary *represents* the restoration and deification, by her birthgiving, of human-kind (once more, *both* men and women) and is not considered, as one theologi-

167. St. Gregory Palamas, "Homilia XXIII: Eis to Dekaton Heothinon Evangelion (Homily 23: On the tenth matins gospel)," in *Gregoriou tou Palama: Hapanta,* Vol. 10, pp. 74, 76.

168. Lossky, *Mystical Theology,* p. 110.

169. St. Irenaeus, *Proof of the Apostolic Preaching,* trans. Joseph P. Smith, S.J. (New York and Ramsey, NJ: Newman Press, 1952), p. 69.

170. *The Philokalia: The Complete Text,* trans. and ed. G.E.H. Palmer, Philip Sher-rard, Kallistos Ware, *et al.* (London and Boston: Faber and Faber, 1981) [hereafter, *Philokalia* (English text)], Vol. 2, p. 294.

52 Chapter Two

cal trend in the Roman Catholic Church would hold, in any sense a Co-Re-
demptrix with Christ or, like Christ (as the Roman Catholic dogma of the Immaculate Conception affirms), to have been Perfect Man, free from sin at her
birth. The celebrated twentieth-century Orthodox churchman, St. John of Shang-
hai and San Francisco, observes, in this regard, that

> [n]one of the ancient Holy Fathers say that God in miraculous fashion purified
> the Virgin Mary while yet in the womb; and many directly indicate that the
> Virgin Mary, just as all men, endured a battle with sinfulness, but was victori-
> ous over temptations and was saved by her Divine Son.[171]

In short, the image of a new Eve in the person of the Virgin Mary is wholly
Christocentric and does not for the Greek Fathers—even if they praise her as the
pure vehicle of the Incarnation, immaculate, ever-virgin (*aeiparthenos*), spotless
and pure in her life and intentions, victorious over her battle with sin, a perfect
image of deified man, "*He Platytera ton Ouranon*" ("She who is more spacious
than the heavens"), and an effective intercessor for her fellow humans—contain
even a hint of co-redemptive Mariological doctrine.

In presenting Christ as the Archetype of the *novus homo* and of Adam and
Eve restored to the Divine course appointed by God, there is present everywhere
in the writings of the early Greek Fathers an unmistakable soteriological leitmo-
tif: that God—Christ—became man, so that man could achieve deification by
Grace. Thus, St. Athanasios the Great (d. 373), tells us, in the characteristic
wording of this universal Patristic axiom, that Christ "enenthropesen hina he-
meis theopoiethomen (was made man, that we might be made God)."[172] The
importance of this aphoristic statement cannot be overemphasized. It contains
within it two essential elements in the deification of man: first, an affirmation of
the restoration of man by his Creator, God Himself; and, second, the indispensable affirmation of the humanity of Christ, Who, while remaining God, at the
same time had to become a true man. This delicate balance between Christ's
Divinity and humanity is a not a trifling matter.

With regard to the Divinity of Christ, the Fathers of the Church teach une-
quivocally that God is unknowable and beyond what is bodily or sensible. Thus,
as one writer, drawing on the theological commentaries of St. John of Damas-

---

171. Blessed Archbishop John Maximovitch, *The Orthodox Veneration of the Mother
of God,* trans. Fr. Seraphim Rose (Platina, CA: St. Herman of Alaska Brotherhood, 1987),
pp. 38-39.

172. St. Athanasios the Great, "Logos Peri tes Enanthropeseos tou Logou (Discourse
on the incarnation of the word)," *Patrologia Graeca,* Vol. 25, col. 192B.

cus, asserts,

> in Holy Scripture 'many things' are said 'concerning God' which are more ap-
> plicable to what is 'corporeal'; but the Saints explain to us that these anthropo-
> morphic expressions should not be taken literally or in their exact sense, but
> 'symbolically': 'Everything that is said of God as if He had a body is said sym-
> bolically, but has a higher meaning; for the Divine is simple and formless.'[173]

The same writer also cites the following words by St. Gregory of Nyssa on the
unknowable nature of God:

> The Divine Word above all forbids that the Divine be likened to any of the
> things known by men, since every idea deriving from some conceptual image
> according to our understanding, which is the product of conjecture about the
> Divine Nature, makes an idol of God and does not proclaim God.[174]

Indeed, in the apophatic tradition of the Orthodox Church, which approaches
God not solely by assertions about what He is, but in terms of His unknowable
Nature, or what He is not (for He encompasses being and non-being alike), "the
divine essence remains in all respects beyond comprehension and participation
(*asylleptos kai ametochos*). Only the uncreated divine energies are accessible
(*prositai*)."[175] About the technical distinction between the Divine Essence and
Energies of God, we will have more to say in the following chapter on Hesychasm. The point here is that,

> [t]o safeguard the doctrine of God's ultimate transcendence of human cogni-
> tion, Orthodoxy makes a hierarchical distinction between 'cataphatic' and 'apo-
> phatic' theologies, which correspond in type to theological affirmations or de-
> nials, respectively. Cataphatically, God is an ultimate and eternal Being; on the
> higher and more 'truthful' apophatic level, however, God is not in essence
> understandable by terms like ultimate, eternal, or Being. God is, in the apo-
> phatic sense, beyond levels of gradation and beyond the categories of time and
> space themselves, since these are but categories appropriate to mere human

---

173. [Archimandrite Cyprian (Agiokyprianites)], "On the Ascension of Our Lord,"
Orthodox Tradition, Vol. 19, no. 2 (2002), p. 2. See St. John of Damascus, *Ekdosis, Patrologia Graeca*, Vol. 94, col. 851AB.

174. *Ibid.* See St. Gregory of Nyssa, "Peri tou Biou Mo[y]seos" (Concerning the life
of Moses), *Patrologia Graeca*, Vol. 44, col. 377B.

175. Romanides, *To Propatorikon Hamartema*, p. 99.

thinking.[176]

St. Gregory Palamas thus insists that the Essence of God "is not a subject for speech or thought or even contemplation, for it is far removed from all that exists and is more than unknowable, . . . incomprehensible and ineffable."[177] Or, as St. Dionysios the Areopagite says of God, He "is above all affirmation . . . [and] . . . , being in His simplicity freed from all things and beyond everything, is above all denial."[178] Vladimir Lossky further contends that the apophatic understanding of God

> teaches us to see above all a negative meaning in the dogmas of the Church: it forbids us to follow natural ways of thought and to form concepts which would usurp the place of spiritual realities. For Christianity is not a philosophical school for speculating about abstract concepts but is essentially a communion with the living God.[179]

As Bishop Auxentios has also observed, in one of our co-authored theological collections, it is not just an understanding of the Essence of God that rests on "negative" theology; the very "doctrine of the Holy Trinity," of God the Father, Son (Jesus Christ), and Holy Spirit, is also "apophatic at heart."[180] Understood in superficial terms, Trinitarian doctrine leads to inane speculation about putative polytheistic tendencies in Christianity (if not, indeed, in some of its heterodox expressions, a subtle but perceptible deviation from the carefully-defined monotheism of Orthodox Christian Trinitarianism). From within the apophatic tradition, and as an experience of the revelation of the True God—as a "theology of facts," to use the words of Father Georges Florovsky—,[181] the Trinity, too, defies mere conceptualization. Rather, it affirms that God in His Essence (and, in fact, in His Energies), is

---

176. Chrysostomos et al., Contemporary Eastern Orthodox Thought, p. 3.

177. St. Gregory Palamas, "Peri Theotetos kai tou Kat' Auten Amethektou te kai Methektou (Concerning non-participation and participation in the Godhead itself)," in Gregoriou tou Palama: Syngrammata, ed. P. Chrestou (Thessaloniki: Royal Research Society, 1966), Vol. 2, p. 242.

178. St. Dionysios the Areopagite, "Peri Mystikes Theologias" (Concerning mystical theology), Patrologia Graeca, Vol. 3, col. 1048B.

179. Quoted in Chrysostomos et al., Contemporary Eastern Orthodox Thought, p. 4.

180. Ibid.

181. [Protopresbyter] Georges Florovsky, Bible, Church, Tradition: An Eastern Orthodox View, Vol. 1 in The Collected Works of Georges Florovsky, 2nd printing (Belmont, MA: Nordland Publishing Company, 1972), p. 120.

indivisibly divided or distinguished into three persons on the basis of origin. The Father is the unbegotten or ungenerated, the Son is begotten of the Father, and the Holy Spirit proceeds from the Father; yet, each of them bears the fullness of the divine nature. The 'how' of the Son's begottenness or of the Holy Spirit's procession is a mystery that is simply unavailable to human understanding. . . . The oneness of the Godhead is preserved by the monarchy of the Father, who is the sole source of [the] divine nature.[182] Yet, . . . the divine nature resides wholly in each of the three persons. . . . There is perfect balance in Orthodox dogma between the threeness and the oneness of God.[183]

At the core of this apophatic understanding of the Triune God is the human experience of God, which, though it involves a "spiritual fact" and a true revelation of God, at the same time insures the utter unknowability of that from which such experience, such facts, and such revelation come forth.

Concerning the humanity of the Divine Christ, the Greek Fathers sedulously point out that the *Theanthropos,* the God-Man Christ, while remaining Perfect God, one with the Unknowable Essence of God, was also Perfect Man, in every way genuinely human, though, by virtue of being God, untainted by the ancestral sin and thus free of the dominion of Satan. As Lossky expresses this quintessential Patristic teaching, God had to become a *true man,* taking on "all that was really human, such as it was after the fall, excepting sin: He took on an individual nature liable to suffering and death." In so doing, He "has assumed also

---

182. This principle led to the rejection, by the Eastern Orthodox Church, of an addition to the Nicene Creed by the Western Church, as early as the fifth century, of the so-called *Filioque* Clause, or what its formulators considered a logical addendum to the Creed: that the Third Person (*Hypostasis*) of the Trinity proceeds from the Father *and the Son* (*Filioque*). From an Orthodox perspective, this addition seriously compromises the unitive monarchy of the Father, subordinating one Hypostasis of the single Trinity. Thomas Aquinas (d. 1274), drawing heavily on the writings of St. Augustine, gave strong support to the *Filioque* Clause in his teachings about the Trinity, in which he posits, among other things, that the Holy Spirit is the love which exists between the Father and the Son. This speculative theology has traditionally been rejected by the Christian East as well, not only on the grounds that love is a manifestation of the unitive monarchy of the Father and thus common to all Three Hypostases of the Triune God, but that the theology of Aquinas and the Latin Scholastics grew out of intellectual exercise and conjecture and not the apophatic theological tradition of spiritual experience and revelation. The theological ideas espoused by the Scholastics also lie outside the consensus of the Greek Fathers, as it is informed by the apophatic tradition.

183. Chrysostomos *et al., Contemporary Eastern Orthodox Thought,* pp. 5-6.

all the imperfections, all the limitations that proceed from sin."[184] The following is a simple but pithily accurate statement of the Patristic teachings on the humanity of Christ, capturing, at the same time, the inseparable Divinity of Christ in His Theanthropic unity:

> He was true God and true Man, or, more specifically, the Person [*Hypostasis*] and nature of God the Son united with the nature of man from His Mother, a daughter of Adam and Eve. As [*sic*] St. Paul confirms His [Christ's] manhood, saying, 'when the fullness of the time was come, God sent forth His Son, made of a woman, made under the law [Gal. 4:4].'
>
> St. Athanasios (296-373) comments, 'Therefore what came forth from Mary, according to the divine Scriptures, was human and the Lord's body was real; real, I say, since it was the same as ours. For Mary is our sister, in that we are all sprung from Adam.'
>
> The two natures would be united without confusion or loss of identity as God or man. The humanity of Jesus was the same as our own and, according to His Divinity, He was of One Essence with the Father and the Holy Spirit.[185]

The perfect Divine and perfect human Natures of Christ, as Lossky further comments, are themselves expressed by the Church Fathers in apophatic terms. In contradistinction to Hellenistic thought, which "could not admit the union of two perfect principles," the Church Fathers understood the two Natures of Christ, "indivisibly and inseparably" united, to be a revealed "mystery" of the kind in which the three Hypostases of the Godhead exist in "one nature." In the apophatic spirit of their theologizing, they not only contained such a truth, but acknowledged that the "'how' of this union remains for us a mystery" that is ultimately "based on . . . [an] . . . incomprehensible distinction," in which "[t]he Divine Person, Christ, has in Him two principles which are different and united at the same time."[186]

The Divine and human Natures of Christ come into focus in the Incarnation and the Resurrection. In the one instance, Christ entered life through a Virgin, the *Theotokos* ("Bearer of God"), was conceived without seed, and came forth from her womb without violating her physical virginity.[187] In the other instance,

---

184. Lossky, *Mystical Theology*, p. 142.

185. [Mother Mariam], *The Life of the Virgin Mary, the Theotokos* (Buena Vista, CO: Holy Apostles Convent, 1989), p. 181.

186. Lossky, *Mystical Theology*, pp. 142-144 *pass.*

187. The idea that the Virgin Mary not only gave seedless birth to Christ, but that she remained physically inviolate in birthgiving, is an ancient and established teaching of the Orthodox Church, even though, in recent times, some writers have questioned it. For

He was crucified, suffered, died, and was buried, while at the same time His death was life-bestowing, transforming both the living and the dead *and* earth and Hades by His Resurrection and victory over death. As was befitting God, Christ was born preternaturally and miraculously rose from the dead; as was befitting man, Christ took human form and was born in a human body, just as He genuinely suffered on the Cross and died. While this focus is of theological import, of course, its anthropological and soteriological significance is immense. By His Incarnation and Resurrection, in which He assumed and deified human flesh, Christ restored man; freed him from the ancestral curse of the pangs of physical birthgiving and (giving assurance that the body and soul would be reunited, after their temporary separation before the full renewal of creation at the end of time and the General Resurrection) the ignominy of bodily death; and provided for human participation in the Divine Energies through His own restorative and transforming participation in the life of the fallen human.

The Incarnation and Resurrection are not simply miraculous events that confirm the Divinity of Christ; they are ontological events that affirm the restoration of human nature. Christ "assumed human nature, gave it its existence, and deified it."[188] It was in recognition of this ontological dimension of the Incarnation and Resurrection of Christ that the Oecumenical Synods that were convoked in the early centuries of Christianity were so assiduous in their efforts to define the theological, Christological, and soteriological precepts of the Church. These were not, for these Synods, matters of semantics or—again, as popular historical and theological prate would have it—the products of a would-be attempt to "create," for allegedly political and social gain, a new religion from the

---

example, Father Thomas Hopko, in his *The Winter Pascha: Readings for the Christmas-Epiphany Season* (Crestwood, NY: St. Vladimir's Seminary Press, 1984), asserts that, beyond doctrinal affirmations that Christ was born supernaturally to a virgin, "there is," in the Orthodox Church, "no teaching of any other sort of miracle in regard to His birth; certainly no idea that He came forth from His mother without opening her womb" (p. 175). As I have pointed out in a review of his book, the one hymnographic reference used by those who support Father Hopko's assertion, does not, when properly translated, actually support his view. In fact, it stands side-by-side with numerous other hymnographic references that clearly and without question attest to the preservation of the *Theotokos'* physical virginity at the birth of Christ. I also point out that, contrary to his counterclaim, numerous Church Fathers and writers, from Justin Martyr to St. John Damascus, uphold this teaching. See Bishop Chrysostomos, review of *The Winter Pascha: Readings for the Christmas-Epiphany Season*, by Thomas Hopko, *Orthodox Tradition*, Vol. 10, nos. 2&3 (1992), pp. 7, 22.

188. Lossky, *Mystical Theology*, p. 142.

rudimentary moral teachings of various messianic Jewish sects. The Synods spoke to events that were central to human restoration and transformation and to the reshaping of the world and the universe. They centered on mega-events that spoke to the convergence of the past, present, and future in the *eternal now* of revealed truth.

The language of the Oecumenical Synods, therefore, is the language of existentialism—striving to protect the lofty profundities of human union with God from the very superficies that are attributed to them by those who reduce Christianity to mere religion and subject it to simple-minded thoughts about human motivation and political and social determinism. The Church Fathers, and especially those who sought to express the teachings of the Orthodox Church about the *Theanthropos,* as Vladimir Lossky concurs, "never lost sight of the question concerning our union with God." That was the primary thrust of the "usual arguments which they bring up against unorthodox doctrines," since "the fullness of our union" with God, human salvation, and "our deification . . . become impossible,"[189] if one succumbs to the theology and Christology of those who deviated from the experiential theological revelation of the Patristic consensus ("heretics," in the Patristic lexicon, or those alienated from the genuine spiritual experience of Christianity and suffering from the pathology of mere religious belief).[190]

---

189. *Ibid.,* p. 154.

190. Interestingly, as Father John Romanides points out, the idea of primacy in Orthodox ecclesiology is also inextricably bound up with the Church's primary task of uniting the faithful to God and assuring "that they may be one, as we are" (St. John 17:11-12). As Romanides asserts, the contemporary ecumenical interpretation of this phrase "is not part of the [Orthodox] Patristic tradition." He maintains that "Christ prays here that His disciples and their disciples may in this life become one in the vision of His Glory (which He has by nature from the Father)." This deifying vision "was part of the Old and New Testament Church's becoming the Body of Christ." Hence, the experience of deification "is the real core of Church history" and the criterion of ecclesial authenticity, and Christ's prayer is "certainly not a prayer for the union of churches." That it should be applied to "churches which have not the slightest understanding of glorification (*theosis*)," he remarks with some irony, "is very interesting, to say the least." Ecclesiastical primacy, in the purest Orthodox Patristic tradition, centers on fidelity to those teachings, doctrines, and observances which lead to holiness and "the cure of the human personality" through union with God "via the purification and illumination of the heart and glorification (*theosis*)." (See John S. Romanides, "Orthodox and Vatican Agreement: Balamand, Lebanon, June 1993," *Theologia,* Vol. 6, no. 4 [1993], pp. 570-580 *pass.*) In another place, Father Romanides even argues that "the abolition of Satan's power" and man's consequent deification and union with God form "the connecting link that gives unity to the Gospels,"

It is perhaps worth noting that Christ was born in the humblest circumstances and without the trappings of earthly royalty that some of the messianic traditions of sectarian Judaism anticipated. To the extent that, disabused of a literal messianic royalty because of the ignobility of these circumstances, we pass beyond the image of "Royal Messianism" to that of "Ontological Messianism,"[191] we come to an understanding that, in the messianic tradition, too, there is a certain conceptual duality. On the one hand, Christians see Christ as the fulfillment of God's covenant with the Hebrew people in their earthly sojourn, extending this Royal Messianism to the messianic catholicity of a "New Israel" (that is, an Israel that includes the non-Jew[192]); on the other hand, the Church Fathers tell us that Christ is the fulfillment of an ontological promise to man, contained within His archetypical revelation of human perfection. Christ was not just the historical Messiah of the Hebrew Covenant, according to Patristic teaching. His Incarnation was, to quote St. Nicodemos the Hagiorite, part of the Divine Oeconomy, "both foreknown and foreordained" by God the Father "prior to the foreknowledge and foreordination of all . . . creatures, both noetic and sensible," which were themselves "both foreknown and foreordained" by the Father "to be created for the sake of the great Mystery of the Incarnation of His Beloved Son." The mystery of the Incarnate Oeconomy, then, is the "foreordained Divine purpose of the origin of existing things."[193] It is "the final end of all things, higher than which there is nothing, . . . [entailing] . . . perfection, deification, glory, and blessedness for Angels, for mankind, and for the whole of crea-

---

chastising "contemporary critics of the New Testament" for their preoccupation with the "inner unity of the Synoptic Gospels" at the cost of the core of the message which they relate in different depths and with divergent catechetical and pastoral aims. (Romanides, *Ancestral Sin*, pp. 71-72.)

191. This is a distinction that I have borrowed, in part, from Father Eugen Pentiuc, though he uses it in a way that moves far beyond my point here. (See Pentiuc, *Jesus the Messiah*, p. xiii.)

192. St. Gregory Palamas underscores this messianic inclusiveness in his comments on the two blind men mentioned in St. Matthew 9:27, who followed Christ, saying, "Thou Son of David, have mercy on us." They signify, he tells us, "the two [human] races, that of the Jews and that of the Gentiles (*ton ex ethnon*)," who were enlightened and thereby recognized Christ as "both God and man." St. Gregory Palamas, "Homilia XXX: Hypothesin Echoun Tous Kata ton Euangelisten Matthaion En Oikia Anablepsantas Typhlous (Homily 30: On the blind men who regained their sight in a house, according to the Evangelist Matthew)," in *Gregoriou tou Palama: Hapanta,* Vol. 10, pp. 263-264.

193. St. Nicodemos the Hagiorite, *Hermeneia eis tas Hepta Katholikas Epistolas* (Interpretation of the seven catholic epistles) (Venice: 1806), pp. 165-166.

tion, . . . the union of the Creator and His creation, and the glory of the unorigi-
nate Father, . . . glorified by His Son and Word, Who clothed Himself in human
nature."[194] We see here both the Royal Messiah of human expectation and the
Ontological Messiah of Divine Oeconomy.

The human condition, as it is expressed in the anthropology and cosmology
of the Greek Fathers, leads one directly to the soteriological scheme which we
have set forth in the Person of Christ as the Archetype of restored man, the Redeemer and Savior of the first Adam, and the Messiah Who, in His ontological
dimensions, is the Creator, the Almighty, and the Ineffable One Who unites the
Creator and His creation. Applied to our investigation of Orthodox psychotherapy, we find in this scheme, from the perspective of human physical and mental
health, an operational definition of what it is that constitutes the "normal" or
"natural" human being—using "natural," in this context, to speak not of fallen
nature, but of the original nature meant by God for mankind. Such a one is he
who, by union with God, restores the perfect connection between the body and
soul, lost through the Fall. As Bishop Kallistos affirms, "since the human person
is a single unified whole, the image of God embraces the entire person, body as
well as soul."[195] The restoration of the image of God in human beings, as well as
their attainment of likeness to God, is therefore directly associated with this connection. "[N]ot only the soul, but also the body of man shares" in this deification, as Lossky also says, "being created, as they are, in the image of God."[196]
"Living . . . with temperance (en metriopatheia)" and "traversing in ease the
period of the present life," the restored man is "delivered" from "the tribulations
of both soul and body" by "Christ Himself, the Physician and God of our souls
and of our bodies," as St. Gregory Palamas tells us.[197]

The normal, or natural and "healthy," state of the human being is also characterized by the Greek Fathers as one of mental deification, which, in turn, is
considered a sine qua non for salvation. Hence, St. Nicodemos the Hagiorite categorically states that, "[i]f your own mind is not deified (theothe) by the Holy
Spirit, it is impossible for you to be saved (na sothes)."[198] This notion of mental
deification, of course, assumes a perfect harmony between body and soul, which
share in salvation and immortality, and in the enlightenment of the nous, or the
spiritual faculty of the mind. Once again, in his natural state, "man is a single

194. Ibid., p. 166, note 1.
195. Ware, The Orthodox Church, p. 220.
196. Lossky, Mystical Theology, p. 116.
197. St. Gregory Palamas, "Homilia XXXI," p. 302.
198. St. Nicodemos the Hagiorite, Nea Klimax (The new ladder) (Thessaloniki: Ekdoseis B. Regopoulou, 1976), p. 247.

totality of soul and body" and it is thus that his deification is accomplished.[199] To a great extent, because of their emphasis on the "eschatological now (*to eschatologikon nyn*)," or the notion that the Incarnation and Resurrection of Christ restored human nature and the universe ontologically, the Greek Fathers hold that this process of deification begins here and now. Through the cleansing of the mind and body, men and women are lifted into a state of deification, such that they live partly, even in the present life, in the future glory of human perfection. In the next chapter, we will address the methodology of this deification: the ways in which the mind is cleansed and the proper relationship between the body and soul is restored. In so doing, we will come to a far clearer idea of what Orthodox psychotherapy is and what it entails.

A Necessary Clarification

To the extent that Western Christians and scholars of religion are familiar with Eastern Orthodox thought—a familiarity varying between none and a great deal, represented by scholarship that ranges from excellent to deplorable—, they often associate the anthropological and cosmological teaching of the Greek Fathers with Platonic, Neo-Platonic, or Gnostic influences. This is partly because the Greek Fathers frequently employ the terminology of classical Greek philosophy. But such an association also too often stems from an inadequate understanding of the tenets and precepts of these classical philosophical schools themselves. For example, St. Gregory Palamas, who is identified with Hesychasm, which we will shortly examine, is incessantly accused of infusing Platonic or Neo-Platonic concepts (which are seldom distinguished from one another with any meticulosity) into his theological writings, when, in fact, a good deal of his philosophical allusions are more Aristotelian than Platonic. (Indeed, his philosophical forte as a student was Aristotelianism.[200]) In any event, the Greek Fathers

---

199. Romanides, *To Propatorikon Hamartema*, p. 125.

200. The story is told of St. Gregory that the Great Logothete of the Byzantine court, Theodore Metochites, when he heard the Saint, as a young student, discussing the logic of Aristotle in the presence of the Emperor, commented: "If Aristotle himself had been present to listen to this young man, he would, I believe, have praised him beyond measure. For the time being, I say that it is those with such a soul and of such nature as his who should be pursuing knowledge, and especially the omnifarious philosophical writings of Aristotle." See St. Philotheos (Kokkinos), Patriarch of Constantinople, "Logos Enkomiastikos eis ton Bion tou en Hagiois Patros Hemon Gregoriou tou Palama (Laudatory discourse on the life of our father among the saints, Gregory Palamas)," in *Hellenes Pateres tes Ekklesias* (Greek church fathers), ed. Panagiotes Chrestou (Thessaloniki:

knowingly and deliberately borrowed the nomenclature of, as well as certain cognitive structures from, Greek philosophy, though with constant declarations that what they had taken from the classical corpus of philosophy they had "baptized" and "transformed" to serve the precepts and tenets of Christianity.[201] Their purpose was not to construct a philosophy of Christianity, fitting it by some frantic Procrustean exercise into the framework of classical Greek philosophy; their stated task was to press the philosophical methods and vocabulary of the ancient Greeks—whom they at times characterized as pagans and bereft of true wisdom—into the service of Christian apologetics and theology. As such, in the words of St. Gregory of Nyssa, Greek philosophy was as if "always in labor but never giving birth."[202]

The arguments that may be brought to bear on those who argue for the undue influence of Greek philosophy on the Fathers of the Eastern Church are many. One may begin with a rather basic observation about charges that the cosmology of the Church Fathers is dualistic. The Greeks Fathers, in concord with Old Testamental Jewish cosmology, as Father Romanides avers, rejected the notion of Hellenistic dualism, which "was wholly alien" to the Jews and to ancient Christian teaching.[203] Elaborating on this point, he writes that, for the Jews, as for the Greek Fathers,

> the world, visible and the invisible, is the only real world created by God for man. Death, for the Jew [and the Orthodox Christian], is not phenomenological but real and tragic. . . . The present world and the future age are not two different worlds. Salvation, therefore, is not salvation from the world but from the present evil. Conversely, for the Greek philosophers, the natural way of salvation is the flight of the soul from the body and matter to the transcendent reality.[204]

The anthropology of the Greek Fathers, too, is wholly at odds with the anthropology of the Platonists, who (along with the Neo-Platonists and Gnostics) would have equated the "resurrection of the body" and its oneness with the soul—anthropological principles basic to the Patristic tradition—"with the damnation of

---

Paterikai Ekdoseis "Gregorios ho Palamas," 1984), Vol. 70, p. 5.

201. See Reverend Gregory Telepneff and Archbishop Chrysostomos, "Hellenistic and Patristic Thought on the *Kosmos* and Man in the Greek Fathers," *Orthodox Tradition,* Vol. 8, nos. 3&4 (1996), p. 12.

202. *Ibid.*

203. Romanides, *To Propatorikon Hamartema,* p. 41.

204. *Ibid.,* pp. 41-42.

the soul, constituting its re-imprisonment [in the body]."[205]

In this vein, Father Georges Florovsky observes, therefore, that "Hellenistic philosophical terms" are "radically transformed in their Patristic" application. As for the alleged influence of Platonic thought on the "Greek Fathers," he argues that they "were actually closer to Aristotle than to Plato," since "Aristotle understood the unity of human existence, of the body and soul, at an intuitive level. . . . [E]mpirical existence and the human personality," for him, "took on an importance that could not be detached from the eternal elements of the soul." Such a concept of human personhood is, of course, wholly foreign to Platonic and Neo-Platonic (not to mention Gnostic) anthropology.[206] Metropolitan John Zizioulas expands on Florovsky's observations with his contention that the Greek Fathers, in fact, synthesized from Platonic and Aristotelian philosophy a vocabulary for talking about the human person that is ultimately contained in neither philosophical tradition:

> Zizioulas observes that Aristotle's notion of man as a psychosomatic entity void of an eternal or permanent quality renders impossible the conceptual union of the 'person' . . . with the 'substance' of man. Thus, Aristotelian man has no true ontology. For Plato, the soul can be united with another physical body; through reincarnation, it can assume another 'individuality' and thus ensure a kind of human, but not unique, personal continuity.[207]

In the Greek Fathers, by contrast, human existence is given an ontological foundation, manifesting those qualities bestowed on it by the Divine Archetype, Christ; that is, the human exists in a unity of person and substance (*hypostasis*). The human being attains to genuine ontology by his participation (*metousia*) and sharing in Divine existence, taking on an eternal dimension for the self. Inarguably, then, the Orthodox Church's understanding of man (and, implicitly, of salvation) diverges essentially and categorically from that of classical Greek philosophy.[208]

Earlier in this chapter, I made reference to various myths about Christianity

---

205. *Ibid.*, p. 42.

206. See Telepneff and Chrysostomos, "Hellenistic and Patristic Thought," p. 16.

207. *Ibid.*, pp. 16-17.

208. This conclusion is given significant support by I.P. Sheldon-Williams, in his investigation of the relationship between Hellenistic and Christian thought. Of particular importance are his chapters in the *Cambridge History of Later Greek and Early Medieval Philosophy*, ed. A.H. Armstrong (Cambridge: Cambridge University Press, 1967), pp. 426ff.

that have made their way from the entertaining speculation of historical pulp fiction to quasi-scholarly status. Many of these myths, as I noted, hold that the early Church fabricated a new religion, subservient to the body politic and bent on controlling man and society. Curiously entwined in this hodgepodge of fables are the foregoing misapprehensions about the influence of Greek philosophy on the Greek Fathers, along with a panoply of fantastic notions about a "shadow" Gnostic Christianity—supposedly suppressed by the Constantinian recognition of the Church—that generally denied the Divinity of Christ, had its own Gospels, preached a form of triumphal feminism, and embraced such Platonic novelties as the pre-existence of souls and reincarnation. These ideas have recently gained attention because of the popularity of such fictional works as *The Da Vinci Code*[209] by Dan Brown, a private secondary school English teacher turned writer, or *The Holy Blood and The Holy Grail,*[210] a wholly fictional work often touted as an "historical work," by Michael Baigent, a conspiracy theorist who holds a degree in psychology, Richard Leigh, a scholar with postgraduate degrees in comparative literature, and Henry Lincoln (né Henry Soskin), an actor and screenwriter. Both of these works try to invoke variant Gospels and arcane historical sources to lend an aura of historical authenticity to what are, in the eyes of some, inappropriate or insipid abuses of sacred personages and, to others, entertaining and, to some degree, clever plots penned by artful writers.

As I have pointed out, early Christianity *was* in many ways inimical to Platonic, Neo-Platonic, and Gnostic beliefs. But this is because Nicene Christianity expressed a consensus confession of the Divinity of Christ. The Nicene Synod was not convened to suppress the views of those who impugned or challenged His Divinity, but to consider disputes that had arisen over the *Nature* of Christ's Divinity vis-à-vis His humanity. Nor, of course, were the pronouncements of the Synod dictated verbatim by a putative non-believer, the Emperor Constantine. Moreover, the Gnostics, who, in this inaccurate scenario are often portrayed as representatives of a more genuine Christianity than that of Nicea, tended to portray Christ through the prism of Docetism;[211] thereby, they both denied His true humanity and considered His body—as well as His suffering on the Cross and death—to be illusions. As for speculation about some hidden feminist agendum in early Christianity, it should be remembered that the very idea of the equality

---

209. Dan Brown, *The Da Vinci Code* (New York: Doubleday, 2004).

210. Michael Baigent, Richard Leigh, and Henry Lincoln, *Holy Blood, Holy Grail* (New York: Delacorte Press, 2005). Published in Great Britain under the title *The Holy Blood and The Holy Grail.*

211. From the Greek word *"dokeo,"* "to seem" or "to appear." Docetism proclaimed Christ to be pure spirit and, therefore, without genuine physical traits.

of men and women—not to mention Jew and Gentile or master and slave—put forth by St. Paul[212] was in and of itself a revolutionary teaching. Strident feminism was as yet just a gleam in the lustful eye of intellectual trends.

Regarding the idea that Christ was married, or the corresponding claim that the Virgin Mary relinquished her virginal purity after giving birth to Christ, such thinking wholly violates the most primitive Christian beliefs, dating to the earliest years of the Church, which upheld a vision, as we have seen, of Christ as the New Adam and the Virgin Mary as the New Eve. The basic assumptions behind this imagery are that fallen man, cursed by the pangs of physical death and reduced, by his misdirected passions, to an act of procreation similar in form to that of an animal, has been potentially restored to a spiritual state, wherein he may transcend the corrupted flesh. Christ as the Archetype of restored humankind and the *Theotokos* as a model for the deification of human beings by their imitation, with the non-physical birth of Christ within them, of her seedless bodily bearing of God—these things are wholly inconsistent with a worldly vision of Christ or His Mother. Additionally, there is absolutely no support for such a vision in the canonical Gospels accepted by the early Church, which date to the first century of Christianity,[213] regardless of the fancies of the Gnostic Gospels, which—as many have forgotten in today's world of historical legerdemain for the sake of promulgating sensationalist conjecture in the service of procuring popular recognition—are later products of the second century.

In the final analysis, the teachings of the Greek Fathers and the pro-

---

212. "There is neither Jew nor Greek, there is neither bond nor free, there is neither male nor female: for all are one in Jesus Christ" (Galatians 3:28-29). Even in an apparent concession to the primacy of his forefathers, St. Paul extends to the Gentiles, in a radical departure from Jewish practice, the covenant of salvation: "[S]alvation to everyone that believeth; to the Jew first, and also to the Greek" (Romans 1:16-17).

213. While many Biblical scholars would like to date the canonical Gospels to the second century, partially in support of the proposition that they have no more historical moment than later uncanonical and dubious texts, the Christian East has always held that the Gospels and the Epistles date to a much earlier period (the Apostolic Age) than Western scholars would admit. In recent times, more and more scholars have given serious attention to the Orthodox dating of Scripture. For example, in one of his more neglected works, John A.T. Robinson came to the astonishing conclusion that, taking all of the extant data into account, the New Testament in its entirety was written before A.D. 70, when Jerusalem fell. (See John A.T. Robinson, *Redating the New Testament* [London: SCM Press, 1976], pp. 336-358, esp.) Jean Carmignac, a Dead Sea Scrolls scholar and expert in Greek and Hebrew, makes a similar argument, through brilliant linguistic analyses, for the dating of the Gospels. (See Jean Carmignac, *The Birth of the Synoptics,* trans. Father Michael J. Wren [Chicago: Franciscan Herald Press, 1987].)

nouncements of the Oecumenical Synods which expressed and defended the spiritual experiences of the early Church are unique unto themselves; stand in contrast to the philosophy of the Greek ancients in whose language they often expressed their theology; and constitute a wholly separate religion from the mélange of Christianity, the various mystery cults, and ancient non-Hebrew religions from which Gnosticism emerged. To study the Orthodox tradition in a fair and punctilious way, one must acknowledge these truths.

Chapter III

Orthodox Psychotherapy: Hesychasm and the Cleansing of the Mind

"Let us implore that it be returned to us,
That second space." *Czeslaw Milosz*[214]

It is axiomatic that Orthodox psychotherapy and the practices of Hesychasm are inextricably linked. This is not because the former is an eclectic phenomenon drawing on a particular "theological tradition" in the Orthodox Church. As we shall see, the precepts and methods of Orthodox psychotherapy correspond perfectly to those of Hesychasm, which, in turn, is simply a recapitulation of the *consensio Patrum,* or that consensual quality of the Patristic corpus that defines the correct teachings of the Fathers and constitutes Holy Tradition (that which has been "handed down"[215]), or the authentic *experience* of human deification by Grace.[216] Thus, Father Georges Florovsky has written about St. Gregory Pa-

---

214. Czeslaw Milosz, *Second Space: New Poems,* trans. Czeslaw Milosz and Robert Hass (New York: HarperCollins Publishers, 2004), p. 3.

215. See Archimandrite [Archbishop] Chrysostomos and Hieromonk [Bishop] Auxentios, *Scripture and Tradition: A Comparative Study of the Eastern Orthodox, Roman Catholic, and Protestant Views* (Belmont, MA: Nordland House Publishers, 1982): "Tradition is the body of doctrines, canons, customs, practices, and artifacts . . . which have been passed on through the centuries in the Church. The Greek *paradosis* also conveys this notion, but includes, in addition, the ideas of 'giving, offering, [and] delivering'" (p. 15). "Tradition is nothing other than the reception, understanding, and interpretation of the Truth" (p. 64).

216. The Patristic consensus is a record of the common experience of the Fathers and their "unified voice, . . . confessing that Christian truth is revealed both through Scripture and Tradition. And the unified voice of the Fathers . . . is nothing more than the 'general conscience of the Church [he genike syneidesis tes ekklesias]'" (*ibid.,* p. 68). It behooves me to emphasize that, for the Church Fathers, Scripture and Tradition (including the writings of the Fathers) do not contain, but simply reveal and enucleate, the common experience of the Church. (Needless to say, the Reformation epithet "*Sola Scriptura*" is unknown in Eastern Christianity and the idea has been dismissed—perhaps rashly or ill-advisedly so—by some theological voices as a form of naïve "bibliolatry.") As Father John Romanides concurs, "[n]either the Bible nor the writings of the Fathers are [the

lamas, the chief defender and formulator of the Hesychastic tradition, that "[a]s a theologian he was simply an interpreter of the *spiritual experience* of the Church." His theology, he points out, was not just dead repetition, but "*was a creative extension of ancient tradition.*"[217] St. Gregory, he further opines, "we may regard as our guide and teacher, in our endeavor to theologize from the heart of the Church."[218] As I have written elsewhere, "the teachings of St. Gregory Palamas constitute a *perfect manifestation* of the catholic, or universal, truth of our Faith[,] . . . the fullness of Christian cosmology, anthropology, and theology."[219] He is a thinker "who belongs to the Eastern Patristic consensus and who expresses the common '*phronema ton Pateron*,' the outlook or 'mind' of the Fathers."[220] Indeed, his genius lay in his singular ability to "assimilate, universalize, and express with remarkable erudition notions of God, man, and the cosmos."[221] Metropolitan Hierotheos also describes St. Gregory as "a traditional theologian par excellence" and as "a bearer of Orthodox Tradition";[222] and Hesychasm he calls "the basis of the dogmas and all the truths of the faith," without which "there is no true theology."[223]

---

actual] revelation or the word of God. They are *about* [actual] revelation and *about* the word of God. . . . [Actual] [r]evelation is the appearance of God to the prophets, apostles, and saints. The Bible and the writings of the Fathers are about these appearances, but not the appearances themselves. This is why it is the prophet, apostle, and saint who sees God, and not those who simply read about their experiences of glorification" (John S. Romanides, *Franks, Romans, Feudalism, and Doctrine: An Interplay Between Theology and Society* [Brookline, MA: Holy Cross Orthodox Press, 1981], pp. 40-41).

217. Florovsky, *Bible, Church, Tradition*, p. 114 (emphasis mine).

218. *Ibid.*, p. 120.

219. Archbishop Chrysostomos, "In Honor of St. Gregory Palamas," trans. Bishop Auxentios, *Orthodox Tradition*, Vol. 17, no. 4 (2000), p. 15.

220. By the "mind of the Fathers," I do not mean a simple agreement in terms and doctrines; rather, this is an expression that refers to "the noetic faculty, the source of spiritual vision for divinized man." See Chrysostomos and Auxentios, *Scripture and Tradition*, p. 72.

221. Bishop Chrysostomos, "Saint Gregory Palamas and the Spirit of Humanism: His Views on Tolerance, Human Dignity, and the Human Body" (paper presented at the Symposium on Byzantine Humanism and Hesychasm, State University of New York at Albany, Fall term 1992). See a revised reprint of this lecture in *Orthodox Tradition*, Vol. 11, no. 2 (1994). The quotation cited appears on p. 8.

222. Metropolitan of Nafpaktos Hierotheos, *St. Gregory Palamas as a Hagiorite*, trans. Esther Williams (Levadia, Greece: Birth of the Theotokos Monastery, 1997), p. 376.

223. *Ibid.*, p. 76.

Notwithstanding these assessments of the status of St. Gregory Palamas, who is extolled and hymned in the Orthodox Church as the "Luminary (*Phoster*) of Orthodoxy," a "Pillar (*Sterigma*) of the Church," and an "invincible Champion of theologians (ton theologon hypermachos aprosmachetos)," and to whom the second Sunday of Great Lent is dedicated, his theological acuity has not always been properly acknowledged. This can be said, ironically (and tragically) enough, of both the Christian West and the Christian East, though, in the latter instance, largely because of the sometimes-noisome effects of Western theological trends on Orthodox thought. In Western Christianity, there is a long tradition of the most extreme hostility towards Palamite thought. Of late, fundamentalist writers have revived the historical animus of various Protestant thinkers towards St. Gregory, drawing, as Alexander Kertzner observes, "rather untenable and crude conclusions" about his teachings, not from "the theological foundations of their Protestant confessional precepts," but on the basis of what he calls their "*religious ideology and pietistic rhetoric.*"[224] For many centuries, Roman Catholic theologians have, on their part, considered St. Gregory to be an "arch-heretic,"[225] though, since the mid-twentieth century, that negative assessment has substantially changed and the associated vituperation has abated. Thus, the Melkite Greek Catholic writer[226] Father George Habra says of Palamas that

> There is scarcely an idea expressed by him of which there is not an approximate formulation in the greatest Fathers, in the most genuine and original currents of thought of the Eastern tradition. No great theologian of the East quotes the Fathers so frequently. . . . The doctrine of Palamas is but the 'organic' development of earlier doctrines, differing from them only in that, while these are very rich intuitions, Gregory has given us a more philosophical and dialectical elucidation of their content.[227]

---

224. Alexander Kertzner, "Protestant Evangelical Theological Ideology: Its Conceptual Deficits Vis-à-Vis Palamite Apophatic Theology," *Orthodox Tradition,* Vol. 23, no. 1 (2006), p. 14.

225. George C. Papademetriou, *Introduction to Saint Gregory Palamas* (New York: Philosophical Library, 1973), p. 20.

226. Greek Catholics (variously called Byzantine Rite Catholics, Eastern Rite Catholics, or somewhat pejoratively Uniates [Uniats]) are members of those Eastern Churches which, while they adhere to the doctrines of the Roman Catholic Church and recognize the Papacy, have their own liturgical rites and customs and are under the governance of their own Hierarchy, which is nonetheless ultimately subservient to the authority of the Pope. Though not in communion with Eastern Orthodox Christians, many Uniates feel a close affinity for the spiritual traditions of the Orthodox Church.

227. Father George Habra, "The Sources of the Doctrine of Gregory Palamas on the

As for the *vexata quaestio* of nugatory criticisms of St. Gregory Palamas and Hesychasm within the Orthodox Church itself, I have noted that these derive primarily from Western influences. Though some authorities dispute the extent of such influences, they were nonetheless clearly pronounced in the Russian Orthodox Church, which was for several centuries preoccupied, to one degree or another, with Roman Catholic (and especially Scholastic) theological systems. In this respect, Father Georges Florovsky writes that Metropolitan Peter of Kiev (Petro Mohyla, 1596-1646) "founded a Roman Catholic school in the Church, and for generations the Orthodox clergy was raised in a Roman Catholic spirit and taught theology in Latin."[228] From this legacy, there developed a manifest disdain for the purer theological traditions of the Orthodox Church, which was reflected in strong anti-Palamite and anti-Hesychastic sentiments. Father Sergey Nedelsky, in his study of the status of Palamite theology in Russia, cites a desk reference book for Russian Orthodox clergy, "officially sanctioned" and published by the Orthodox Church of Russia in 1913, that addresses the teachings of Hesychasm under a section "dedicated to 'Schisms, Heresies, Sects, Etc.'" The comments contained in the entry for "Hesychasts" mimic the accusations of Palamas' Latin critics and chief antagonist, the Calabrian Uniate monk Barlaam (to whom we will return subsequently). "Hesychasts" are portrayed as "monastic mystics" in fourteenth-century Greece who taught that "by lowering their chin towards the chest and gazing at their navel they would see the light of Paradise and rejoice in seeing celestial inhabitants." The entry goes on to point out that the Hesychasts considered "quiet ... concentration ... an indispensable condition for the perception of the uncreated light," a "nonsensical opinion" that purportedly faded into "oblivion on its own."[229]

It would be wrong to leave the impression that what we have said about the denigration of Hesychasm and the purer theology of the Orthodox Church in Russia held forth in monastic circles. The monastic estate never wholly severed

---

Divine Energies," *The Eastern Churches Quarterly,* Vol. 12, no. 6 (1958), p. 245.

228. [Protopresbyter] Georges Florovsky, *Ways of Russian Theology: Part One,* Vol. 5 in *The Collected Works of Georges Florovsky* (Belmont, MA: Nordland Publishing Company, 1979), p. 72.

229. [Rassaphore-monk] Sergey Nedelsky, "Palamas in Exile: The Academic Recovery of Monastic Tradition," M.Th. thesis, St. Vladimir's Orthodox Theological Seminary, 2006, p. 18. See Sergei Vasilevich Bulgakov, *Nastol'naia Kniga dlia Sviashchenno-Tserkovno Sluzhitelei* (Desk reference book for sacred ecclesiastical servers), 3rd edition (Kiev: Tipografiia Kievo-Pecherskoi Uspenskoi Lavra, 1913), p. 1622 (translated passages from the entry in Bulgakov's desk reference book are those of Father Sergey).

its ties to Hesychastic spirituality; nor did it generally embrace the anti-Palamite spirit of academic theology. Moreover, in the contemporary Russian Church, a rehabilitation of Palamite thought is certainly underway—and has been for many decades. Therefore, a work on the Russian Orthodox Church published just several years before the fall of the Soviet régime, while perhaps not elaborating on the *pivotal importance* of Palamite theology, discusses "the spreading in Rus of the religious-philosophical doctrine of hesychasm, which came from Byzantium" and which was "evolved by Gregory Palamas, a hermit of Mt. Athos." It also acknowledges that Hesychasm had a direct effect on coenobitic (communal) monasticism in fourteenth- and fifteenth-century Russia (a claim that other Russian scholars have also made for the influence of Hesychasm in general on Russian monasticism[230]).[231] In addition, the widespread renaissance of interest in,

---

230. See John Meyendorff, "The Metropolitanate of Russia: From Kiev to Moscow," chapter 8 in Aristeides Papadakis, *The Christian East and the Rise of the Papacy: The Church 1071-1453 A.D.* (Crestwood, NY: St. Vladimir's Seminary Press, 1994), pp. 341 ff. *pass.*

231. Ya. N. Shchapov, "Christianity and the Church in the 12th-14th Centuries," chapter 3 in *The Russian Orthodox Church: 10th to 20th Centuries,* ed. Alexander Preobrazhensky and trans. Sergei Syrovatkin (Moscow: Progress Publications, 1988), p. 55. Not entirely extraneously, let me observe that this book is one of the last specimens of Soviet propagandistic writings about the religious traditions of Russia. Particularly illustrative of such works are the comments, in chapter thirteen, by N.S. Gordienko on the Russian Orthodox Church Outside Russia, the ecclesiastical jurisdiction formed in the diaspora, after the Bolshevik Revolution, by Orthodox clergy and faithful fleeing the anti-religious policies of the Communist régime. This body was for many decades known in the Russian émigré community for its criticism of collaboration, before the fall of Communism, between the Church administration in Russia and the Soviet authorities and for a strong rooting in spiritual traditions deeply influenced by Hesychasm. However, Dr. Gordienko describes the Russian Orthodox Church Outside Russia as discouraging "the strengthening of ecclesiastical tendencies" among the faithful, for fear of compromising its purportedly purely "political" agenda (i.e., anti-Communist activities). Quoting "one of the leaders of the Russian Orthodox Church" (without identifying him or providing a citation), he claims that, "engrossed in their mundane concerns," the ecclesiastical principals of the Church "do not know the doctrine of the Orthodox Church" and have "no interest for [*sic*] it." He also quotes the Church's "Hierarchy" (once again, without citation and without identifying his source) as admitting that "membership in Orthodoxy" is for them "of purely formal significance" ("The Russian Orthodox Church Abroad," p. 444). (Very recently, I might note, these two parts of the Russian Orthodox Church have initiated a process of reunification.)

Of equal interest is chapter ten, "The Church Under the New Social Conditions," by

and positive attention to, the teachings of St. Gregory Palamas and of Hesy-chasm can be attributed, in great part, to the theological investigations and writings of Russian theological thinkers in the diaspora. These individuals (e.g., Archbishop Basil Krivocheine [d. 1985], Father Alexander Schmemann [d. 1983], Father John Meyendorff [d. 1992], and Father Georges Florovsky) brought Hesychasm into a new eminence and helped to bring Palamite thought out of its Western captivity—albeit with differing rates of success and various levels of disengagement from the fetters of Western theological thought.

It was not only in the Russian Church, but in the Greek Church, as well, that Western influence—from both Latin and Protestant quarters—contributed to the obnubilation of the centrality of Palamite thought in Orthodox theology.[232] Curi-

---

Gordienko and Dr. M.P. Novikov. In it, the authors portray the Russian Orthodox Church under communist rule as responding to the "urgent need . . . for renovating certain traditional dogmatic definitions" and embracing the "flexibility" necessary in "theological dialogues with Catholic and Protestant theologians." While admitting that "the content of [Orthodox] Christian dogmata could not be changed," the authors assert that the Orthodox Church in Russia has been able, nonetheless, to rethink and restate some of the "most obsolete elements of Orthodox dogmata" (p. 340). In addition to revising "the Orthodox interpretation of the dogma on the Church" (p. 343), we are told that, "in 1971," at the "Third Local Council of the Russian Orthodox Church," the Council members "sanctioned the Church's support for the socialist social and state system" (pp. 346-347). This move the authors contrast to their curious assumption that traditional Orthodox doctrine, substituting "divine determination" for the communist dogma of "social determination," reduces "social values" to a "level of purely moral values"—"the choice between good and evil"—and the quest for "holiness" in Christ. Human freedom, they argue, is likewise debased in Orthodox thought to matters of "grace and predestination" (the latter a doctrine foreign to Orthodox Christianity) or "obligatory love for God" (another concept inimical to Orthodox teachings) (pp. 324-325). With respect to our discussion of Orthodox psychotherapy, such crude theological misstatements represent the survival, under the yoke of Soviet ideology, of a deviant kind of theological thought that led to the misinterpretation of Hesychasm by Russian churchmen under the yoke of Westernization. Indeed, the comments about the Russian Orthodox Church Outside Russia, aside from their political content and propagandistic intent, also reveal an insensitivity to the legacy of the Hesychasts, since, in their pejorative references to the internal life of that Church, the authors wholly ignore this characteristic and widely-acknowledged aspect of its witness.

232. Professor Chrestou observes pointedly, with regard to the influence of both Protestant and Roman Catholic theology on the Greek Church, that "Greek theology, since its new formation in the beginning of the nineteenth century [i.e., after the Greek Revolution], was entangled by a tragic adventure. Its heart was rooted in Orthodoxy, its mind was fed by Protestantism, and its argumentation derived from scholasticism." See Panagiotes K. Chrestou, "Neohellenic Theology at the Crossroads," *The Greek Orthodox*

ously enough, as Russian theologians in the diaspora began to shake away the fetters of Western theological captivity, they came face to face with what Professor Giannaras calls a spirit of "formalism" in the theology of the other national Churches, and particularly the Church of Greece. Criticizing this spirit in Greek academic theology in an article written more than thirty years ago, Giannaras notes that "a theologian of the faculty of Athens," reacting to the revival of the apophatic tradition—the "mystical theology of the Eastern tradition, . . . so-called Neo-Palamite theology," or Palamite Hesychasm[233]—in Russian theology, "wrote that apophaticism, since in itself it signifies a negation, is inadmissible for Orthodox theology."[234] He was not captious in expressing his objections to the reaction of the theologian in question, since late nineteenth-century and a good deal of twentieth-century Greek theology suffered, as I have indicated, from theological ideas and theories of Western and heterodox provenance that clearly did damage to the integrity of its traditions, even if these traditions survived, as in Russia, to some degree in monastic communities. Fortunately, a "Patristic revival"—a "renewal," as Giannaras calls it—was already underway among Greek intellectuals at the time that he penned his complaints about theological formalism in Greek academic theology.[235] It was that revival which led

---

Theological Review, Vol. 28, no. 1 (1983), p. 51. Professor Giannaras, summarizing the distortions introduced into Greek ecclesiastical life by the lay brotherhoods that proliferated in Greece in the early twentieth century and subsequently, decries the "abolition of the holy icons" and their replacement by Renaissance art, "the almost exclusive use of Roman Catholic and Protestant manuals and religious literature," and various "polemics against monasticism and the Holy Mountain," the latter, of course, an historical bastion of Hesychastic spirituality. See Christos Yannaras, *The Freedom of Morality*, trans. Elizabeth Briere (Crestwood, NY: St. Vladimir's Seminary Press, 1984), p. 135.

233. Christos Yannaras, "Theology in Present-Day Greece," *St. Vladimir's Theological Quarterly*, Vol. 16, no. 4 (1972), p. 207.

234. *Ibid.,* p. 204.

235. *Ibid.,* p. 205. Giannaras numbers among those (aside from himself) who were at the "forefront" of the "renaissance within . . . Greek theology" at the time that his article appeared, Professors Nikos Nissiotis, John Zizioulas (now Metropolitan of Pergamon), Panagiotes Chrestou, and G. Mantzarides (pp. 208-209). He likewise mentions a number of scholars outside the Greek faculties of theology whose works played a significant role in this theological renaissance. One would also have to mention, in this circle, Father John Romanides, who was so deeply influenced by his mentor at Harvard University, Father Georges Florovsky, and the many theologians who were either formed by, or drew from, the theological writings of Romanides, including Father George Metallinos, Metropolitan Hierotheos Blachos, and other prominent theological figures whom I cite in this work.

to a rebirth of academic interest in, and renewed spiritual enthusiasm for, Hesychasm and, ultimately, to the emergence of the idea of Orthodox psychotherapy
in Greece.

St. Gregory Palamas: His Life and Times

Before examining Hesychastic theory and its method of human restoration,
I should make some brief comments about the life of St. Gregory Palamas. He
was born at the end of thirteenth century, the scion of a noble Byzantine family.
His father was an advisor to Emperor Andronicos II (Palaeologos) and a Sena-
tor, and St. Gregory was reared and educated, under the direction of the Emperor
himself, in the environs of the court. Deeply pious from his youth, at twenty
years of age he retreated to Mt. Athos, where he entered the monastic life. (It is
worthy of note that, like his father, who was tonsured a monk shortly before his
death, his mother, under Gregory's influence, became a monastic, as did his two
brothers and his two sisters.) On Athos, the young monk excelled in a spiritual
life marked by numerous supernatural experiences and visions. In 1326, he was
ordained a Priest in Thessaloniki. He also founded a monastic community in
Berroia (near Thessaloniki), not long after his ordination. In 1347, he was con-
secrated Archbishop of Thessaloniki, where he reposed twelve years later. During his life, the Saint suffered a number of hardships on account of his defense
of Hesychasm. He was imprisoned for his teachings, in 1344, on the orders of
the Patriarch of Constantinople. He languished in captivity for almost four years.
He was also taken captive by the Turks, for a short period of time, during his
many travels. In 1368, Gregory was "proclaimed" a Saint, or "glorified,"[236] by a
Church Council held at Constantinople, nine years after his repose,[237] bringing

---

236. Technically, the Roman Catholic term "canonization" does not apply to the process by which Saints are recognized in the Orthodox Church, where Sainthood grows out
of the popular veneration of holy personages. The Church's public "proclamation" or
"announcement" of the inclusion of such individuals in the calendar of Saints constitutes
a validation by the entire Church of this veneration, which often first occurs informally at
a local level.

237. See the full life of St. Gregory in Philotheos (Kokkinos), "Logos Enkomiastikos."
A brief life of the Saint, drawn from this work, can be found in Metropolitan Hierotheos,
St. Gregory Palamas, pp. 29-58. Also see an extensive biography of Palamas and a detailed commentary on his theology in Monachos Theokletos Dionysiates, *Ho Hagios
Gregorios ho Palamas: Ho Bios kai he Theologia Tou 1296-1359* (St. Gregory Palamas:
his life and his theology 1296-1359) (Thessaloniki: P. Ginnoules, K. Tsolerides, G. Dedouses, 1984).

to a close the life of one of the Orthodox Church's most significant figures, whose theology, in the strictest sense, should not be called "Palamite theology," as one authority correctly states, but simply "the theology of the Church."[238]

In bringing together his own remarkable life experiences, spiritual accomplishments, and witness with the Church's teachings on human deification—"the ultimate aim and purpose of human life" as it is "defined in the Patristic tradition"[239]—, St. Gregory Palamas was very much a man of his age. He flourished in the century after the tragic conquest of Constantinople by Roman Catholic Crusaders—when, from 1204 to 1261, the Patriarchate there, "for all intents and purposes," was "simply united to the Papacy by forced conversion" under its Latin captors[240]—and died almost a century before the collapse of the Byzantine Empire to the Turks in 1453, which followed a desperate attempt by the Byzantine Church, in 1439, to court Western military alliances against the Turks by a hasty and ultimately futile union with Rome. Hence, it was a direct confrontation between the traditions of the Christian East and the ascending influence and power of the Papal monarchy and Scholasticism in the Christian West which sparked the theological controversy to which Palamas responded with his philosophical and dialectical statement and defense of Hesychasm.

The controversy regarding Hesychasm, which raged for more than a decade and a half, beginning in the mid-1330s, was instigated by the monk Barlaam (*vide supra*), who arrived in Byzantium sometime around 1330.[241] He was supported in his opposition to Palamas by several "Latin-*minded*"[242] contemporaries of the Saint, foremost among them the monk Gregorios Akindynos, who, at one time a friend of St. Gregory, "had initially tried to mediate the dispute between Palamas and Barlaam" but "subsequently criticized" Palamas "on the grounds that he had distorted Patristic tradition," further condemning him as an "innovator."[243] (Some historians have suspected that Akindynos' desire to be appointed to the Archbishopric of Thessaloniki, to which Palamas was instead appointed,

---

238. Metropolitan Hierotheos, *St. Gregory Palamas,* p. 381.

239. Florovsky, *Bible, Church, Tradition,* p. 114.

240. Archbishop Chrysostomos, *Orthodox and Roman Catholic Relations from the Fourth Crusade to the Hesychastic Controversy* (Etna, CA: Center for Traditionalist Orthodox Studies, 2002), p. 133.

241. Father Theokletos of the Dionysiou Monastery on Mt. Athos places Barlaam's arrival at around 1326. Monachos Theokletos Dionysiates, *Ho Hagios Gregorios,* p. 43.

242. This term—"*Latinophron*" in Greek—was used during the era in question to describe Orthodox intellectuals, theologians, and clergy who had fallen under the sway of Roman Catholic theology and, in particular, Latin Scholasticism.

243. Chrysostomos, *Orthodox and Roman Catholic Relations,* pp. 208-209.

partly accounted for his change in heart towards St. Gregory and the Hesychasts.[244]) The other most notable opponent of St. Gregory was the Byzantine
philosopher and scholar, Nikephoros Gregoras. Gregoras "was not pro-Latin,"[245]
and it seems that his recusancy and vehement antipathy towards St. Gregory,
which landed him in prison (where he died), stemmed from his *inability to understand* Palamas' teaching on the Nature of God.[246] However, it was Barlaam
who best represented, in his dispute with the Saint, the confrontation of the mystical theology of the Orthodox East and the rationalism of Latin Scholasticism
that the Hesychastic controversy actually was. It was also Barlaam who fabricated the anserous charges that the Hesychastic tradition on Mt. Athos, in which
St. Gregory was trained, taught a system of "navel-gazing (*omphaloskopia*)" and
physical exercises that allowed one to see the "Essence of God," thereby falling
to Messalianism (a fourth-century heresy holding that the Persons of the Trinity
were visible to the human eye). And it was in response to Barlaam's sometimes-
inane charges that the vast majority of St. Gregory's writings were written.

I might note that a number of Western scholars, joined by not a few Orthodox theologians, have argued that Barlaam was not the antagonist that St. Gregory Palamas took him to be and that the Palamite controversy was not the clear
confrontation between Orthodox theological thinking and Western Scholasticism that it is made out to be. One such writer is Father John Meyendorff, whose
works, while instrumental in bringing Palamite theology to the attention of contemporary Western scholars, have also perpetuated some unfounded assumptions about the dispute between Barlaam and St. Gregory. Many of these are
contained in his most popular book on Hesychasm, *Introduction à l'Étude de
Grégoire Palamas*.[247] Father John Romanides has written an incisive review of
this work, discussing in detail its deficits. His critical remarks form a prism
through which any serious student of St. Gregory's theological writings must
read Meyendorff's Palamite scholarship.[248] Meyendorff and other investigators,
Father Romanides points out, are too often "over-impressed by Barlaam's 'anti-
Latin' works" and thus downplay his Scholastic leanings and the fact that, after

---

244. *Ibid.,* p. 210.

245. J.M. Hussey, *The Orthodox Church in the Byzantine Empire* (Oxford: Clarendon
Press, 1990), p. 259.

246. Chrysostomos, *Orthodox and Roman Catholic Relations,* pp. 209-210.

247. Jean Meyendorff, *Introduction à l'Étude de Grégoire Palamas* (Introduction to
the study of Gregory Palamas) (Paris: Éditions du Seuil, 1959).

248. Reverend John S. Romanides, "Notes on the Palamite Controversy and Related
Topics," *The Greek Orthodox Theological Review,* Part I, Vol. 6 (Winter 1960-61); Part
II, Vol. 9 (Winter 1963-64).

the Hesychastic controversy had come to an end, he "return[ed] to the Latin Church, where he became a Bishop."[249] The fact is that Barlaam, although of Greek blood from Calabria in Italy, "was," as the Athonite monk Father Theokletos avers, "a Greek Uniate" from "the ranks of those Calabrian monks . . . who accepted the commemoration of the Pope." Theokletos further speculates that Barlaam made his appearance in the Byzantine capital to work for the union of the Orthodox Church with Rome.[250]

Romanides shares Father Theokletos' suspicions about Barlaam. He argues that Father Meyendorff and other scholars fail to consider

> The question [of] why Barlaam came East and then worked for union with the West, especially in view of [his] . . . acting as though the Christians of Byzantium were plunged into ignorance. At first the Calabrian gave the impression that he came East convinced that the Greeks possessed the true faith; but then he worked hard and passionately for union [with Rome] by way of compromise. An explanation of these two facts, either in terms of the traditional Byzantine suspicion that Barlaam was a Latin spy, or in some other terms, is certainly to be expected.[251]

In view of the questions that Romanides raises, it seems reasonable to speculate that Barlaam did, indeed, make his way East—whether as an ecclesiastical *agent provocateur* or on some personal quest—for the purpose of minimizing the spiritual differences between Eastern Orthodoxy and Western Catholicism. If that is true, it is not farfetched to imagine that he found it expedient to attack and denigrate the one tradition that starkly brought the differences between the Christian East and West into focus: Hesychasm. Barlaam's harsh criticisms of the Hesychasts were answered with exemplary patience and kindness by St. Gregory Palamas. Thus, in closing his first letter to the Calabrian, the Saint praises Barlaam's wisdom and assures him that, despite the seriousness of his errors, he is still viewed with love.[252] By contrast, Barlaam "called" the Hesychasts "many derogatory names" and "distorted and ridiculed the Hesychastic doctrine as it was practiced in [the monasteries of] Mt. Athos,"[253] leading one to think that the Calabrian's provocative and contumelious language, which helped to fan the fires of discord, was not *in effect,* at least, that of an agent of peace

---

249. *Ibid.,* Part I, p. 193.
250. Monachos Theokletos Dionysiates, *Ho Hagios Gregorios,* pp. 44-45.
251. Romanides, "Notes on the Palamite Controversy," Part I, pp. 193-194.
252. *Gregoriou tou Palama: Hapanta,* Vol. 1, p. 512.
253. Papademetriou, *Introduction to Saint Gregory,* p. 23.

and a man of dialogue. Whatever the case, it was, again, at his instigation that the Hesychasts, in the person of St. Gregory Palamas, formulated their apologetic statement of the Church's teachings on divinization.

Palamas on Hesychasm, Prayer, and the Deifying Knowledge of God

It is not my purpose here, in what I intend as a *guide* to Orthodox psychotherapy, to provide an exhaustive examination of the complex theology of Hesychasm that underlies that therapeutic method, any more than my foregoing chapter on Orthodox anthropology, cosmology, and soteriology was meant to cover in anything but a cursory manner the vast conceptual territory of Orthodox theology. Nor can I even *hope* to approach, in my summary of Hesychastic teaching, a cyclopedic consideration of the voluminous works and profoundly intricate theological system of St. Gregory Palamas. My purpose is simply to present the basic precepts and practices of Hesychasm that emerged from the Hesychastic controversy in fourteenth-century Byzantium. To that end, let me begin by defining the words "Hesychasm" and "Hesychast." These terms derive from the Greek word for "silence" or "stillness": "*hesychia.*" Thus Hesychasm ("*hesychasmos*") is the practice of silence and the Hesychast ("*ho hesychastes*") one who follows this practice, striving thereby to achieve "interior stillness and freedom from passions" and to render his or her prayer "limpid purity";[254] or, as Metropolitan Hierotheos states, Hesychasm is "the practice of stillness in the presence of God" and "those who practice it are called hesychasts."[255] I should emphasize that to call Hesychasm "Quietism" and its practitioners "Quietists," as some uncareful scholars do, is misleading. Technically, these words apply to a sect founded by the seventeenth-century Spanish monk Miguel de Molinos (1628-1696).[256] Despite certain superficial parallels in terminology and practice,

---

254. Constantine N. Tsirpanlis, *Introduction to Eastern Patristic Thought and Orthodox Theology* (Collegeville, MN: The Liturgical Press, 1991), p. 7.

255. Metropolitan Hierotheos, *St. Gregory Palamas*, p. 394.

256. Molinos was heavily influenced by the piety and writings of the sixteenth-century Spanish Catholic Saints, Teresa of Ávila and John of the Cross. He taught a system of passive contemplation (hence, "Quietism"). Molinos died in prison, after his condemnation for heresy by the Congregatio Sancti Officii, or the "Holy Office," the body originally established by the Inquisition for examining the orthodoxy of doctrine and practice in the Roman Catholic Church. (As an aside, there has arisen of late the bizarre theory that Molinos may have been condemned by the Holy Office because his teachings were influenced by Jewish Kabbalah. This theory is based on his affinity for the mysticism of

Molinos' Quietism is wholly at odds with the precepts of Hesychasm. Professor Constantine Tsirpanlis writes specifically about Hesychasm as a practice that it is

> [a] system of Christocentric mysticism . . . and [of] psychosomatic . . . practices—especially . . . perfect quietude of body and mind (to attain the vision of the Uncreated Light of God)—of Eastern ascetics (since the Fourth century Desert Fathers) known as the *hesychasts of Mt. Athos* (Greece), where even today they are found . . . , [who] follow the same life-style . . . [as] . . . their chief founder, . . . St. Gregory Palamas (1296-1359). Hence, this type of monasticism is [also] called . . . *Palamism*, the deepest 'communion and union with God' through the 'Jesus Prayer' or *Cardiake prosefché*, the outgrowth of Christ's love.[257]

This short description provides us with a précis of Hesychastic practice and a clear enumeration of the themes that St. Gregory Palamas addresses in his apologetic writings. Quite correctly, Tsirpanlis traces Hesychasm back to the Desert Fathers. In tracing the *Hesychastic controversy* itself to Mt. Athos, however, he perhaps inadvertently leaves the incautious reader with the impression that its practice is not universal to Orthodoxy. In fact, Hesychasm "was not . . . an Athonite phenomenon or something peculiar to Mt. Athos (though, assuredly, its practice and defense cannot be separated from the experience . . . of that paradigmatic monastic republic)."[258] Nor was it a purely "domestic issue" for the Athonites, as one Western authority opines,[259] or "a retreat into an ivory tower of spiritual and cultural rationalism" or obscurantism, as yet another Western scholar claims.[260] Regarding the specific themes that Tsirpanlis enumerates in

John of the Cross, whose father, Gonzalo de Yepes, came from a wealthy Spanish family with Jewish roots. Such a link with Kabbalah is very unlikely and wholly unsupported by any real data.) Molinos' *Guía Espiritual* (Spiritual guide), in which he presents his method for attaining, as the full title of the work states, "[el] rico tesoro de la interior paz ([the] rich treasure of interior peace)," was published at the beginning of the last century in English translation (from the Italian version of the work, *Guida Spirituale*). See Miguel de Molinos, *The Spiritual Guide Which Disentangles the Soul,* ed. Kathleen Lyttelton (London: Methuen, 1907).

257. Tsirpanlis, *Introduction to Eastern Patristic Thought,* p. 7.

258. Chrysostomos, *Orthodox and Roman Catholic Relations,* p. 201.

259. Joseph Gill, *Byzantium and the Papacy* (New Brunswick, NJ: Rutgers University Press, 1979), p. 204.

260. Kenneth M. Setton, *The Papacy and the Levant, 1204-1571* (Philadelphia: American Philosophical Society, 1976), Vol. 1, pp. 42, 310, note 187.

his description of Hesychasm, these are primarily the concerns set forth in Palamas' famous defense of the Hesychasts, "Hyper ton Hieros Hesychazonton (On
behalf of the sacred hesychasts)," which was probably "written between 1338
and 1341."[261] This work is comprised of "nine treatises" in the form of questions
and answers. "Because they are arranged in groups of three [in three parts], they
have been dubbed his *Triads*."[262] The entire work constitutes a general response
to the charges leveled chiefly by Barlaam against the Athonite Hesychasts.[263] As
the eminent Byzantinist Joan Hussey contends, these are basically theological
and Patristic defenses of the idea—so repulsive to Barlaam—that "both here and
in the next world man . . . [can] . . . share in God through uncreated energies."[264]

In his work on the Hesychasts, St. Gregory confronts the Scholastic philosophical proclivities of Barlaam, pointing out that spiritual knowledge comes,
not through mere education or worldly knowledge, but through the radiance that
results from the cleansing of the mind (which then resides in the heart) and the
attainment of holiness and Apostolic virtue: "Phaneron toinyn hos hyper logon
te kai gnosin aute he ellampsis (It is thus apparent that this radiance is above
human intellect and knowledge)."[265] Mere worldly knowledge, to which Bar-

---

261. Others argue that the text was more likely composed between 1337 and 1339. See
"Introductory Remarks," *Philokalia* (English text), Vol. 4, pp. 290-291.

262. Chrysostomos, *Orthodox and Roman Catholic Relations,* p. 207. The discourses
can be found in *Gregoriou tou Palama: Hapanta,* Vol. 2, pp. 56-725.

263. Among the other works by the Saint that touch on Hesychasm, or the Hesychastic
controversy directly, are his letter on Hesychastic practice to the Nun Xenia (*Gregoriou
tou Palama: Hapanta,* Vol. 8, pp. 348-431), composed, according to Professor Chrestou,
in 1342 (*ibid.,* p. 54); three very brief treatises on Hesychastic prayer and the centrality
of the heart in Orthodox spirituality (*ibid.,* Vol. 8, pp. 264-271), thought by most authorities to predate the Hesychastic controversy and dated by Chrestou to 1333 (*ibid.,* p. 36);
his one hundred fifty discourses on theology and the ascetic life, in which the Saint provides a complete outline of Orthodox cosmology and anthropology, as well as a refuta-
tion of Akindynos' misunderstanding of the Essence-Energies distinction and the meaning of *theosis,* or human deification (*ibid.,* Vol. 8, pp. 74-261; also found in Vol. 150 of
the *Patrologia Graeca*), which work Chrestou does not date, but which was probably
written in the last decade of the Saint's life; and the "Tomos Hagioreitikos (Hagioritic
tome)," which St. Gregory wrote in 1340, on behalf of the monastic leaders of his time on
Mt. Athos, who signed it and who affirmed, with their approbation of the text, that the
Saint was, indeed, not an innovator writing about some eccentric personal set of beliefs,
but was faithfully expressing the prevailing Hesychastic traditions of the Holy Mountain
(*Gregoriou tou Palama: Hapanta,* Vol. 3, pp. 496-515).

264. Hussey, *The Orthodox Church,* p. 258.

265. *Gregoriou tou Palama: Hapanta,* Vol. 2, p. 258

laam attributed salvation, the Greek Fathers—St. Gregory says—find vain and even evil or demonic. He goes on to argue that Barlaam's argument against pure prayer, or prayer which is accomplished by concentrating the mind in the heart ("en to tes charitos throno [in the throne of Grace]"), which is the *"tameion* (repository)" of the Holy Spirit,[266] is based on a misunderstanding of the body. Barlaam and his followers, in arguing that the mind should be freed from the body in prayer, contradicted, in the view of St. Gregory, the Pauline doctrine that the body is the temple of the Holy Spirit within man (I Corinthians 6:19). When the mind is cleansed of sin and passions, Palamas affirms, it functions in concord with the body; one sees in himself "ten epengelmenen charin tois kekatharmenois ten kardian (the Grace promised to the pure in heart)."[267]

When the essence of the mind (the *nous*), which is actually a faculty of the heart (or the soul),[268] establishes a natural relationship with the heart, the heart comes to exercise control over one's thoughts (and thus the discursive intellect), and the mind becomes "watchful" (from the Greek *"nepsis,"* or "vigilance," "watchfulness"—hence the term *Neptikoi Pateres* [or "Neptic Fathers"], which is often applied to the Hesychasts). This relationship is aided, St. Gregory Palamas teaches, by such physical exercises as the control of the breath and the rhythmic recitation of the "Jesus Prayer"[269] in conjunction with the breath. The body, he reminds us, must participate actively in prayer, facilitating the return of the mind to the heart. The concentration of the mind, in silence and stillness, on the center of the body (the navel) or on a candle, and the consequent removal of distractions during the recitation of the Jesus Prayer, St. Gregory says, in re-

---

266. *Philokalia,* Vol. 4, p. 125.

267. *Ibid.*

268. See Chapter II, "The Anthropology of the Greek Fathers," above. A discussion of the diverse ways in which the term *"nous"* is used in Scripture and the Patristic corpus can be found in Metropolitan Hierotheos, *Orthodoxe Psychotherapeia*, Section 2, "Schese Metaxy psyches, noos, kardias, kai dianoias (logikes) (The relationship between the soul, *nous,* heart, and discursive intellect [rationality])," pp. 111-115. He admits that there is significant "confusion" in the way that the term is variously used (*ibid.,* p. 112). I prefer to follow the definition cited from Larchet in the designated section of Chapter II, above, which is adequate for our discussion of the cleansing of the mind in Hesychastic spiritual practice.

269. The "Jesus Prayer" exists in several forms. The most familiar formula is, "Lord Jesus Christ, Son of God, have mercy on me, a sinner." It is sometimes shortened to "Lord Jesus Christ, have mercy on me," or even "Lord, have mercy on me." Though not a substitute for the Jesus Prayer, St. Gregory Palamas was fond of a similar devotional entreaty, "Photison mou to skotos (Enlighten my darkness)."

sponse to Barlaam's accusations of *omphaloskopia* (navel-gazing)—or corollary proclamations that the Athonite Hesychasts were *"omphalopsychoi"* (from the Greek words for "navel" and "soul"), or individuals who believed that the soul resided in the navel—, are "aids" in returning the mind to the heart and achieving the knowledge of God which is contained therein. Moreover, through this kind of psychosomatic concentration, the Hesychasts are able to achieve a profound level of prayer—*prayer of the heart*—that leads to the integration of thought and spiritual knowledge, enlightening the mind and bringing the body and soul into perfect harmony.

Following the attainment of pure prayer, St. Gregory Palamas tells us, one becomes, through an intimate knowledge of, and encounter with, God within the heart, a true theologian. It is, indeed, at this point in spiritual development that the spiritual aspirant for the first time begins to understand Scripture and its spirit. In addition, the Saint speaks even of *physical reactions* to pure prayer. As Metropolitan Hierotheos notes, "the heart itself leaps for joy at the coming of Grace, and frequently a pleasant taste is created in the mouths of those who pray . . . [;] and this is the energy of divine Grace."[270] But more importantly, pure prayer leads to the vision of God, Who manifests Himself in what Palamas calls *"aktiston phos* (Uncreated Light)" or the *"theia ellampsis* (Divine Radiance)" of God. This Light, he maintains, was the same Light in which Christ appeared in Mt. Thabor at the Transfiguration.[271] It was also the Divine Light that St. Paul experienced on the road to Damascus, as an "arrabona tou kat' auten endymatos (pledge of [our] investiture therein)."[272] The mystical vision of Uncreated Light floods the mind with Grace, such that the spiritual mind (again, the noetic faculty or *nous*, the very essence of the mind) is totally cleansed and "liberated by the power of the Holy Spirit," as Romanides asserts, "from the influences of both the body and the discursive intellect."[273] The body being thus "freed from sin" and "controlled by the mind [*nous*], which becomes its overseer (*he episkope*[274]),"[275] no longer do "the physical and intellectual faculties ... ex-

---

270. Metropolitan Hierotheos, *St. Gregory Palamas,* p. 69.

271. "Kephalaia Hekaton Pentekonta Physika kai Theologika, Ethika te kai Praktika kai Kathartika tes Barlaamitidos Lymes (One hundred fifty chapters on natural and theological, ethical, and practical topics, and issues purgative of the Barlaamite scourge)," *Gregoriou tou Palama: Hapanta,* Vol. 8, p. 158.

272. *Ibid.*

273. Romanides, "Notes on the Palamite Controversy," Part II, p. 229.

274. *Philokalia,* Vol. 4, p. 124.

275. Chrysostomos, "Saint Gregory Palamas and the Spirit of Humanism," p. 17.

ercise any influence whatsoever on the noetic faculty."[276] Instead, "they are . . . dominated by the noetic faculty's unceasing prayer [and] are spiritually cleansed and inspired and at the same time may engage in their normal activities."[277]

It is in his discussions of the vision and knowledge of God as Uncreated Light that St. Gregory Palamas explains the Essence-Energy distinction, in response to the accusations of Barlaam that, like the Messalian heretics, the Hesychasts claimed to achieve a physical vision of God by beholding what they considered His Essence (*ousia*). Barlaam explained this as an apparition of light and the product of "created Grace," in keeping with the Augustinian tradition that prevailed in Scholastic theology.[278] In the first place, everywhere in his writings in defense of Hesychasm, St. Gregory makes it clear that the Hesychasts, unlike the Messalians, do not strive for a physical vision of the transcendent, unknowable Godhead (i.e., to a vision of the unseen *Essence* of God); nor do they claim, he says in response to Barlaam's charge to that effect, that the Uncreated Light of God is His unknowable Essence. Such nonsensical charges, egregious examples of the kind of vapid calumny in which Barlaam often engaged (a deficit that even those somewhat sympathetic to him admit[279]), are most effectively addressed in the "Hagioritic Tome." There, St. Gregory declares that the Uncreated Light which the Hesychast sees, when he comes to a knowledge of God, is a manifestation of the Energies of God, which are perceived by the spiritual mind (the noetic faculty) and, indeed, by the senses, but only after the latter have been

276. This is why knowledge of God comes not from intellectual pursuits and is not dependent, *per se,* on them, as Romanides says, echoing the words of Palamas.

277. Romanides, "Notes on the Palamite Controversy," Part II, p. 229.

278. In contradistinction to the idea of knowing God through created apparitions of Grace, Romanides argues that, whereas "[f]or Barlaam, knowledge of God is rational . . . , [f]or Palamas knowledge of God is based on the suprarational experience of the prophets, apostles, and saints; it transcends all rational knowledge. . . . These observations indicate strongly that in the persons of Barlaam and Palamas one is confronted with a real clash between the *credo ut intelligam* of the post-Augustinian West and the apophatic theology of the Greek Fathers." (See Romanides, "Notes on the Palamite Controversy," Part I, p. 191.) In many ways, as Father Romanides acknowledges, Barlaam and Palamas were arguing past one another, working, as they were, from theological ideas about God's Essence, about Grace, and about spiritual knowledge that, beyond terminology, had little in common at the conceptual level.

279. Father John Meyendorff, for example, whom Romanides accuses of being uncritical of the Calabrian's anti-Orthodox sentiments, admits that Barlaam had a "proud temperament" and an "aggressive spirit," and that he was "intractable." See Meyendorff, *A Study of Gregory Palamas,* trans. George Lawrence, 2nd edition (Leighton Buzzard, England: The Faith Press, 1974), p. 46.

purified, transformed, and illuminated by the return of the spiritual mind to the heart, wherein the mind is illumined by Divine Grace. In the oft-quoted words of St. Gregory, this spiritual knowledge and vision of God transcend both the senses (and the discursive intellect) and even the noetic essence of the mind, deriving, as they do, from the same vision of "the glory of God revealed in this life to the patriarchs, prophets, and apostles."[280]

Barlaam strongly challenged the Patristic provenance of this teaching, as did Akindynos, accusing St. Gregory of "innovation." Aside from what we have already said about the concord between Palamite teaching and the consensus of the Greek Fathers, suffice it to quote, with regard to the Essence-Energies distinction, the following from Metropolitan Hierotheos:

> To be sure, this [doctrine] did not originate with St. Gregory but is the teaching of the entire Orthodox Tradition, for the Apostolic Fathers referred to the subject of the distinction between essence and energy in God, and we see it again in the teaching of St. Basil the Great.[281]

The Calabrian argued that, by the Essence-Energies distinction, St. Gregory had posited the existence of two Gods—a crude conclusion that was taken up (albeit in a more nuanced manner) by Gregoras. Palamas' answer to Barlaam was that both God's Essence and His Energies are uncreated and that the distinction between them preserves both the ability of man to achieve divinization *and* God's absolute unity and unknowability. Through God's Energies, as Papademetriou, puts it, "[w]e attain participation in the divine nature, and yet it remains *totally inaccessible*."[282] In other words, St. Gregory differentiates God's Essence from the deifying Energies which those who have experienced deification recognize and know as the "'manifestations' and [uncreated] 'exteriorizations' of God."[283]

---

280. Romanides, "Notes on the Palamite Controversy," Part I, p. 194. Cf. *Gregoriou tou Palama: Hapanta*, Vol. 3, p. 510: "Hotan de pneumatikes kai hyperphyous eumoiresosi charitos te kai dynameos, aisthesei te kai no ta hyper pasan aisthesin kai panta noun hoi katexiomenoi blepousin (When they have achieved spiritual and supranatural Grace and power, those who have been so vouchsafed behold both sensibly and noetically that which is above all sense and intellect)."

281. Metropolitan Hierotheos, *St. Gregory Palamas*, p. 305.

282. Papademetriou, *Introduction to Saint Gregory*, p. 43.

283. *Ibid.* Father Papademetriou is quoting, here, Archbishop Basil Krivocheine. I have added the word "uncreated" to modify the word "exteriorization," since one must not understand this word to suggest any kind of "created" or merely "sensible" manifestation of God.

That this distinction is essential to the soteriology of the Orthodox Church and its teachings on the deification of man, Giannaras clearly affirms: "The West," and Barlaam, "rejected the distinction, desiring to protect the idea of simplicity in the divine essence." As he explains, for the West, "the energies of God are either identified with the essence" of God or with some "created result of the divine cause," as Barlaam maintained. As a consequence, Giannaras correctly observes, "the *theosis* of man, his participation in the divine life, is impossible, since even grace, the 'sanctifier' of the saints, is itself an effect, a result of the divine essence." Fundamentally, man's divinization, "even though supernatural," is thought to be "created . . . , as Western theologians have arbitrarily" held "since the ninth century."[284] Without the Essence-Energies distinction, then, the entire structure of Orthodox teaching on the divinization of man in direct and intimate knowledge of God—the precise aim and the goal of the Hesychast—collapses.

The Cleansing of the Mind and the Hesychastic Method of Human Restoration and Deification

The process by which humankind is restored "presupposes above all," as Metropolitan Hierotheos remarks, "that the noetic faculty of the soul"—the essence of the mind or, as Larchet puts it, the "image of God in man" and the "indelible mark" of man's "true nature"[285]—"should be healed."[286] As we have observed, this course of healing begins with the return of the mind, through meditative concentration aided by the recitation of the Jesus Prayer, silence or stillness, and the control of the breathing, to the repository of Divine Grace in the heart. There, attaining to the vision and knowledge of God in Uncreated Light, the mind is freed from the control of sin (the human inclination to move away from the perfection for which men and women were created), from the thoughts and distractions of the discursive intellect, and from the passions of the body. Flooded by the Divine Light of the vision of God, the human being restores in himself unity between the body and soul and begins to function in such a way as to facilitate his ascent, *in this life,* to perfection. It is this process that Father John Romanides identifies with Orthodox tradition and the Greek Fathers:

---

284. Christos Yannaras, "The Distinction Between Essence and Energies and Its Importance for Theology," *St. Vladimir's Theological Quarterly,* Vol. 19, no. 4 (1975) pp. 242-243.

285. Larchet, *Thérapeutique des Maladies Mentales*, pp. 37-38.

286. Bishop Hierotheos, *Orthodox Psychotherapy*, p. 138.

Orthodox tradition presents a method for the curing of the mind of man;
that is, of his soul. This therapy entails two aspects . . . , enlightenment and deification. Deification—that is, the vision of God—is the guarantor of a cure, of a
total cure [of the mind]. This therapeutic method, or therapeutic regimen, that
the Orthodox tradition presents is handed down . . . from generation to generation, born by individuals who have attained enlightenment and deification and
became therapists for others. That is, it is not a simple transmission of knowledge from books, but a transmission and succession of experience, a succession
of enlightenment and deification.[287]

Before examining the precise methodology of Orthodox psychotherapy, I
would like to make a few comments on Father Romanides' important observations about these core teachings of Orthodoxy. First, he once again confirms the
irrefragable unity of Hesychastic theory and practice with the historical experience of Eastern Orthodoxy as far back as the age of the Apostles and the era of
the Desert Fathers; and, beyond that, even with the lives of the "Patriarchs and
Prophets of the Israelites," who also attained to enlightenment and deification.
The tradition of enlightenment and deification "did not suddenly appear from
nothing . . . in the eleventh or twelfth century after Christ,"[288] Romanides insists;
Hesychasm *is* the very tradition of Orthodox Christianity and of its Old Testamental precedents. Second, Romanides' words help us to understand why "Orthodoxy is not," as he further says, "a religion" as such ("one among the many
religions"), and why it does not have "as its *central* concern the preparation of
the members of the Church for life after death, to ensure, thereby, a place in
Paradise for every Orthodox Christian." Nor, as he goes on to say, does it exist
merely for the purpose of insuring that those who accept "Orthodox dogma" will
not "go to Hell." Similarly, the teachings of the Fathers are not, according to
him, ultimately divided between spiritual traditions which teach, on the one
hand, that this life is *solely* a "preparation for life after death" or, on the other
hand, that religion exists to provide man with a way to avoid tribulation in this
life and to receive from God all that one "needs" and "desires."[289] These lower
aspects of religious concern—matters of cognitive or confessional and doctrinal
origin—seek, in the words of the brilliant expounder on Halakhic man in Jewish
thought, Rabbi Joseph Soloveitchik, "to transform the secrets embedded in crea-

---

287. Protopresbyter John S. Romanides, *Paterike Theologia* (Patristic theology) (Thessaloniki: Ekdoseis Parakatatheke, 2004), pp. 39-40.

288. *Ibid.,* p. 40.

289. *Ibid.,* pp. 42-48 *pass.* (emphasis mine).

tion into simple equations that a mere tyro is capable of grasping." In the higher pursuits of the spirit, he tells us, "the *homo religiosus* is intrigued by the mystery of existence—the *mysterium tremendum.*"[290]

---

290. Rabbi Joseph B. Soloveitchik, *Halakhic Man,* trans. Lawrence Kaplan (Philadelphia: The Jewish Publication Society, 1991), p. 7. Let me say, here, that Soloveitchik further contrasts the *higher* religious pursuits of *homo religiosus* with the *highest* pursuits of Halakhic man, who, like the Hesychast, is focused on the reality of this world, finding himself "free of any element of transcendence" and thus "orient[ing] himself to reality through a priori images of the world which he bears in the deep recesses of his personality" (or, in Hesychastic parlance, in the recesses of his person) (*ibid.,* p. 17). I do not wish to overstate, to the point of conceptual and theological abuse, the similarities between Halakhic man and the Hesychast; but neither do I wish to ignore the fact, as Romanides often points out, that there persist in Jewish mysticism, too, many of the elements of holiness that the Hesychastic tradition envisions and, to be sure, also attributes to the Jewish Patriarchs and Prophets. Therefore, one is not wholly surprised by a reference by Gershom Scholem, in his foundational study of Jewish mysticism, to the Kabbalistic doctrine of the *Neshamah,* or the "soul proper," as it is presented in the *Sefer Ha-Zohar* (or *Book of Splendor*), an important mystical text composed in Spain in the late thirteenth century. In this work, the *Neshamah* is presented as "the deepest intuitive power" in man, "which leads to the secrets of God" and "is also conceived as a spark of *Binah,* the divine intellect itself" (Gershom Scholem, *Major Trends in Jewish Mysticism* [New York: Schocken Books, 1995], pp. 240-241). Again avoiding speculation about parallel development, the similarities between the the *Neshamah* and the *nous* are too obvious to be ignored.

In a fascinating guest lecture delivered by Martin Jaffee for a recent Spiritual Life Institute program at St. Martin's University in Lacey, WA, Professor Jaffee commented on Jewish monastic piety, which, as he points out, "existed in Judaism during the second Temple period, roughly from 150 B.C.E." to "the end of the first century C.E." (p. 2). Connecting monasticism and mysticism, he avers that the ascetic spirit of Jewish monastic piety survives in Halakhic Judaism's spiritual disciplines, marked as they are by a) "limits" placed on the "physical enjoyment of creation" through b) "a system of behavioral restraints" that c) "impose upon personal awareness" and d) lead to "a sense of perpetually standing in the Divine Presence. . . . In this four-fold sense, a person engaged in Halakhic discipline is in constant awareness of the body's physical demands, one's own psychic resistance or capitulation to them, and of the fact that, while one's struggle may be internal, it is acted out in a community before God" (p. 5). (Martin Jaffee, "Mysticism and Monasticism: A Perspective from Judaism" [paper presented at the Spiritual Life Institute, St. Martin's University, Lacey, WA, June 2006].) While we must, once again, exercise caution and not draw imprudently concrete parallels, we find here, too, compelling evidence of the presence in Halakhic spirituality of principles not unknown to Hesychasm and which the Hesychastic Fathers, as we have observed, find in the witness of the Jewish Patriarchs and Prophets.

With respect to its absolutely *essential* goals—even beyond the concerns of the *homo religiosus*—, Orthodoxy as a *way of life* is centered on the "cleansing, enlightenment, and deification" of man. The Fathers of the Church focus "on this world, on this life," and on the restoration of man. "Be he Orthodox, Buddhist, or Hindu, be he an agnostic or an atheist," from the "Orthodox theological point of view," Romanides says, "the destiny of every man on earth is to see the Glory of God," which "Christ first reveals to man in this life" (i.e., to those who "decide . . . to follow . . . the path of [spiritual] therapy") and which "all men" will see at the *Parousia,* or "the Second Coming of Christ." The goal of the Church is to help determine *"how"* each man will see that Glory: whether "as Light" or as "a consuming fire,"[291] in keeping with the extent to which he has achieved, by following the spiritual methods of the Church, a true vision of God—enlightenment and deification—in this life. Though heterodox and foreign ideas have eroded this traditional and Patristic understanding of the Orthodox Church and the spiritual life, this is the Church as Orthodox theology properly expresses it.

It is partly because Barlaam did not understand Orthodoxy to be more than a religion that he kindled and became embroiled in the Hesychastic controversy. If, as some suspect, he went East from Calabria to achieve a union between Eastern Orthodoxy and Roman Catholicism, it well may be that he was motivated wholly by his confessional adherence and a desire to unite the Orthodox "heretics" to the "true Church." Thus, he could not possibly have understood the Hesychasts, who were not thwarting his aspirations on account of some sort of theological or confessional intractability, but because their spiritual lives and practices were not a matter of speculative theology but of *spiritual experience.* Like chemists confronting an alchemist, the Hesychasts, in response to Barlaam's outrage at what he saw as conceptual and theological heresies in their precepts, found his wholly speculative Scholastic theories "heretical" because they deviated from the established *empirical experience* of the Greek Fathers. Moreover, his views they considered "demonic," since they were not aimed at what they took as the goal of all *true religion*—the restoration of man to the image of God—, the obfuscation of which constituted, for them, the work of Satan. Thus, Barlaam and the Palamites were speaking with terms that they differently defined: of theology as an intellectual exercise and an aspect of religious confession, on the part of Barlaam; and, on the part of the Hesychasts, as an imperfect expression of an *empirical spiritual experience.* We have, here, a clash between religion and theology as ways of coming to an intellectual know-

---

291. Romanides, *Paterike Theologia,* pp. 46-49 *pass.*

ledge of God over and against religion as a "therapeutic way of life" and theology as the spiritual data of those, to quote Metropolitan Hierotheos, who have been "initiated" into the mysteries of the Faith "by actual experience."[292]

I have already mentioned in a fairly general way some aspects of Hesychastic methodology in my references to prayer of the heart: the use of the Jesus Prayer in stillness, concentration on the center of the body (the navel) or a candle, control of the breath, and the exercise of vigilance or watchfulness over thoughts. Since my aim is to offer a basic overview of Orthodox psychotherapy, and not to provide a detailed guide to Hesychastic practice (which should, as its practitioners universally asseverate, *never be undertaken* without the manuductive ministrations of an accomplished spiritual advisor), I will simply outline other practices which play a role in Hesychastic practice, though, again, without specific practical details. Nonetheless, I would like to stress at the outset of this endeavor that the practice of Hesychasm is not an abstract form of contemplation or a psychic method for the attainment of celestial visions; it entails practical efforts in the form of physical, as well as mental, exercises.

Indeed, the very purpose of Hesychastic prayer is to avoid *extraneous* thoughts and distractions—setting aside all "evil thoughts" and "suspending external stimulation."[293] It is by controlling one's thoughts and ceasing to seek external things, in the pure contemplation of God through the Jesus Prayer, that we accomplish "[t]he entry of the mind into the heart," where "the mind not only collects its thoughts, but examines and reflects upon itself. . . . It enters the Kingdom of God within." In this process, "it 'sees itself' (*'heauton ho nous hora'*[294])" in the "grace-filled inner chamber" of the heart and thus comes to a spiritual state which is above the "desultory spiritual experiences that we encounter in contemporary 'mysticism'" or merely ecstatic "spiritual encounters."[295] Hesychasm is, as I noted above, closely connected to a psychological process and to a *practical* way of life. Thus, even the monastic community or the Church, for the Hesychast, is not just "an association of pious people" seeking social fellowship or sharing some mystical vision of Heavenly profundities. The monastic institution—or a parish—"is a spiritual Hospital which heals man." In it, we find the "uncured in soul . . . , those who are being cured," and, in addition, the "Saints of the Church," who "are . . . already cured."[296] "Christianity" itself is, in its essence, something *practical:* "a therapeutic treatment"; and its clergy are not

---

292. Metropolitan Hierotheos, *St. Gregory Palamas,* p. 318.

293. Bishop Hierotheos, *Orthodox Psychotherapy,* pp. 138, 139.

294. *Philokalia,* Vol. 4, p. 126.

295. Chrysostomos *et al., Contemporary Eastern Orthodox Thought,* p. 56.

296. Archimandrite Hierotheos, *The Illness and Cure of the Soul,* p. 81.

those who "issue tickets for Paradise," or guides in some mystical journey into disembodied bliss, but "therapists" with an active role in the "cure" of the souls entrusted to them.[297]

At the root of the practical life of the Hesychast is a regimen of ascetic observance by which he separates himself from those thoughts, passions, and distractions that cloud the mind—of ascetic pursuits that help to cleanse the essence of the mind and to purify the body, which comes to serve the soul: "Cleansing the body of all sinful thoughts, we make it the abode of spiritual power, ruled over, appropriately, by the mind." Thus ruled, "the body is not an evil thing, but a thing of good"; it becomes "a spiritual instrument."[298] This "[a]scesis," Father Metallinos writes, "is the spiritual struggle which is laid down and conveyed by the Tradition of the Church."[299] As Metropolitan Hierotheos says,

> The transformation of man is not limited to the transformation and alteration of the soul [mind or *nous*] alone, since . . . man is soul and body together. The body must also take part in the journey to deification, because it too will be glorified. . . . If we limit our struggle to our soul alone and do not extend it to the body as well, we can stumble into rupture, with traumatic consequences. St. Gregory Palamas repeatedly points out that we need the spiritual armour of watchfulness and prayer for the nous, and of continence for the body.[300]

Among the ascetic practices[301]—the "method of therapy"—that Metropolitan Hierotheos sets forth are fasting, vigils, and prayer. To these can be added *enkrateia* (temperance and moderation) in monitoring and controlling the senses

---

297. *Ibid.,* p. 91.

298. Chrysostomos *et al., Contemporary Eastern Orthodox Thought,* pp. 54, 55.

299. Metallinos, "The *Exomologetarion* of St. Nicodemos," p. 22.

300. Metropolitan Hierotheos, *St. Gregory Palamas,* pp. 133-134.

301. With regard to ascetic practice, I would like to stress that, in Hesychasm, it is not undertaken in the spirit of a contemptuous disdain for the world (*contemptus mundi*). When the Hesychasts speak of the folly and vanity of the world and disdain for it, they are speaking of the untransformed world and the experiences of the untransformed human being. Asceticism, as we shall see subsequently, in our discussion of fasting, is positive and restorative. Moreover, it is, as Father Florovsky points out, not something that "blinds creativity." Rather, he says, "it liberates it, because it asserts it as an aim in itself. Above all—creativity of one's self. . . . Ascesis does not consist of [mere] prohibitions. It is activity, a 'working out' of one's own self. It is dynamic. . . . [T]hrough the ascetic, the very vision of the world is changed and renewed." [Protopresbyter] Georges Florovsky, *Christianity and Culture,* Vol. 2 in *The Collected Works of Georges Florovsky,* second printing (Belmont, MA: Nordland Publishing Company, 1974), pp. 127-128.

and passions, moral uprightness, proper and virtuous Christian comportment, following the commandments of God, almsgiving, good works, and a life centered on the Mysteries of the Church. By these means, all of which are prescribed by the Neptic Fathers, one achieves, through Divine Grace, enlightenment.

Fasting in the Orthodox Church and in the Hesychastic tradition involves not just the control of the types and quantity of food eaten, but also the commemoration of certain spiritual entities or personages and of sacred events in the liturgical year. Orthodox monks and nuns—who as a rule do not eat meat—fast on most Mondays, Wednesdays, and Fridays (in commemoration of the Angels, Judas' betrayal of Christ and the Cross [or in honor of the *Theotokos*[302]], and the Crucifixion, respectively) from fish, dairy products, and olive oil, while Orthodox lay persons follow a similar fast on Wednesdays and Fridays, avoiding, in addition to all that monastics eschew, meat as well. There are other very long fasting periods (forty days or more) of varying strictness appointed in preparation for Pascha, in commemoration of the Apostles, in honor of the Dormition (what Roman Catholics call the Assumption) of the Virgin Mary, and in preparation for the Feast of the Nativity of Christ (as Christmas is properly called in the Orthodox Church). Fasting for married couples also includes "fasting from the flesh" (abstinence from sexual relations) on fasting days and during lenten periods. It is also "connected with prayer," as Metropolitan Hierotheos affirms, with the "submission of [the] personal will" to "the Church, . . . Christ and the holy Fathers of the Church, who have decreed" that one should fast, and with the "control of the senses."[303] Fasting is not a matter of deprivation and self-punishment; it represents the restoration of the obedience of Adam and Eve to the prohibition that they "not . . . eat of the tree of the knowledge of good and evil," the violation of which "resulted in man's death."[304]

Vigils, or night prayers and long periods of isolation and spiritual reflection, are closely associated with fasting, involving, as they do, bodily discipline. They

---

302. For example, in his book of services for each day of the week, the famous hymnographer, Father Gerasimos of the Little Skete of St. Anne on Mt. Athos (hence his monastic appellation, "Mikragiannanites"), dedicates Wednesdays to the Mother of God. Monk Gerasimos Mikragiannanites, *Hebdomadarion: Parakleseis kai Charetismoi tes Hebdomados* (Weekly service book: Supplicatory canons and salutations for the week) (Holy Mountain: 1987), pp. 89-105.

303. Metropolitan Hierotheos, *St. Gregory Palamas,* p. 137.

304. *Ibid.,* p. 136. Bishop Kallistos makes this same observation in his commentary, "On the Meaning of the Great Fast [i.e., the lenten period before Pascha]": "One of the primary images in the Triodion is that of the return to Paradise" (*The Triodion*, p. 46).

are sometimes accompanied by spiritual reading and, in some instances, the chanting of Church hymns and Psalms. Vigils also typically include a struggle against sleep (or at least excessive sleep), though always, as in all Orthodox asceticism, only "when the body is strong,"[305] since the purpose of asceticism is to bring the body under control and not to harm or punish it. *Enkrateia,* or self-controlled moderation, addresses the negative emotions—evil thoughts, jealousy, resentment, anger, etc.—that are inspired in man by the influence of Satan, as well as the fleshly temptations and sexual concupiscence that arise from the distortion and transformation of spiritual love for God *(eros)* into lust and sexual desire.[306] Moral uprightness and proper and virtuous Christian comportment are acquired, according to the Greek Fathers, by a conscious imitation of the virtues of Christ, the Apostles, the Martyrs, and the Saints, who serve as models of purified and deified man. Their examples of self-abnegation, humility, concern for others, love, and sacrifice serve to inform the spiritual aspirant about, and to inspire him to emulate, the life of holiness—the "way-method by which we attain to communion with God."[307] As for almsgiving[308] and good works, these are

---

305. Metropolitan Hierotheos, *St. Gregory Palamas,* p. 154.

306. It is not the consensus teaching of the Greek Fathers that sexual desire is evil—though it *is* a characteristic of post-Lapsarian man—or that human sexuality is repugnant or contemptible. Rather, they constitute, as I have said, a degraded and distorted form of the human longing for God. When controlled within a life of ascetic struggle and sexual purity (celibacy) or confined to the Mystery of marriage (wherein physical love is elevated by the Grace of the Church), the sexual impulse can be transformed and restored to its original function: that of drawing man—though not by compulsion or even the power of the "irresistible grace" of Western Christian theological thought—to the love of God. Father James Thornton and I discuss this subject in some detail in our book *Love,* Vol. 4 in *Themes in Orthodox Patristic Psychology* (Brookline, MA: Holy Cross Orthodox Press, 1990), esp. pp. 61-68.

307. Archimandrite Hierotheos, *The Illness and Cure of the Soul,* p. 179. In a wonderful essay on the comportment of Hesychastic practitioners, Hieromonk Klemes notes that one who is a true Christian sees his "brother as an image of God, worthy of honor, attention, forbearance, forgiveness . . . [and] love." He further states that, "[i]t is good for us to be radiant and to have a smile on our face before we speak, and to show genuine joy over the successes and accomplishments of our neighbor and genuine sorrow over his afflictions and trials." Hieromonk Klemes (Agiokyprianites), "Genuine Nobility: Monasticism and Sociability," *Orthodox Tradition,* Vol. 23, no. 2 (2006), p. 6.

308. About the restorative power of almsgiving, St. John Chrysostomos (d. 407) says, "Oude gar houtos hydatos physis aponiptei kelidas somatos, hos eleemosynes dynamis aposmechei rypon psyches (Indeed, the property of water does not wash away the stains of the body as much as the power of almsgiving purges the defilement of the soul)." See

both disciplines in the cure of the soul *and* fruits thereof. It is for this reason that the Orthodox Church has never entered into the debate over salvation by works or by Grace that became a matter of major contention between Roman Catholicism and the Protestant Reformers. The Greek Fathers—who have, for one thing, a far different view of salvation than most Western Christians—recommend, on the one hand, the performance of good works as part of a disciplined effort to acquire Grace and, on the other hand, acknowledge good works as the natural, spontaneous activity of those who, transformed by Grace, act in synergy with God.

With regard to the Mysteries (sacraments) of the Church, the Orthodox Patristic consensus and Hesychastic teaching have typically approached them from within a medical model; i.e., as psychic or spiritual remedies. The Eucharist, for example, is often called by the Greek Fathers the *"Pharmakon Athanasias* (Medicine of Immortality)."[309] Thus, as Panayiotis Nellas, calling the Eucharist "the center of the spiritual life," notes, in it, "the whole person in all its dimensions, with all its psychosomatic senses and functions, is joined in a deep union with Christ."[310] This idea of curative restoration also characterizes Baptism—or, as it

---

his third homily on II Corinthians 4:13 ("Peri eleemosynes [On almsgiving]"), *Patrologia Graeca,* Vol. 51, col. 300.

309. See, for example, this term as it is used in the first century by St. Ignatios of Antioch (d. *ca.* 107), "Pros Ephesious (To the Ephesians)," *Patrologia Graeca,* Vol. 5, col. 661A.

310. Panayiotis Nellas, *Deification in Christ,* p. 127. It is worthy of note, here, that the entire Hesychastic tradition places immense importance on the Eucharist. The champions of Hesychasm on Mt. Athos in the late eighteenth and early nineteenth centuries (among them, St. Nicodemos the Hagiorite), who are often exclusively associated with a liturgical dispute, in their time, over the appropriate day for commemorating the dead, were actually more actively involved in "a return to a Eucharistic-centered spirituality and the precepts preached by the Hesychasts in the fourteenth century." (See Hieromonk Patapios and Archbishop Chrysostomos, *Manna from Athos: The Issue of Frequent Communion on the Holy Mountain in the Late Eighteenth and Early Nineteenth Centuries* [Oxford: Peter Lang Publishing, 2006], p. 30.) Meyendorff, in his commentary on the homilies of St. Gregory Palamas, avers that Palamas and the Hesychastic Fathers placed great emphasis on the Eucharist as the "seul moyen de recevoir en soi la vie divine (the sole means of taking into oneself the divine life)." (Meyendorff, *Introduction à l'Étude de Grégoire Palamas,* p. 396.)

While not arguing against the centrality of the Eucharistic Mystery in Hesychastic spiritual practice, Romanides takes exception to the attribution, by Meyendorff, to Palamas of what he calls "incarnational and sacramental mysticism." Father Romanides suggests that Father Meyendorff was "evidently . . . embarrassed by the Greek Patristic insis-

was also known in the ancient Church, *"photismos* (illumination)," the initial enlightenment of the *nous* by Mysteriological purification—and all of the Church's
Mysteries. Even in services of exorcism, which confront the entanglement of the
human mind (if not the body) in the *real* evil of Satanic and human resistance to
the Divine Will (and it is in Satanic and human disobedience, again, and not in
God, that evil resides), the Church intervenes to *cure* the mind and soul of the
malevolent darkness of Satan and his minions and the bacterium of human sin.
As I have written elsewhere,

> The disjunction of mental processes from a clear and healthy vision of the natu-
> ral state of man—whether because of distorted religious belief, a complete ca-
> pitulation to the passions and the lower side of human nature, or even a bio-
> chemical or organic disorder—leads, in the teaching of the Eastern Church Fa-
> thers, to what we would today call 'mental illness' [i.e., the darkening of the
> mind]. Satan and demonic powers hold full sway over such persons.[311]

In the same way that the Hesychastic disciplines of "fasting and prayer" are effective in "repelling satanic attack[s]"[312]—the darkening of the mind by Satan's

---

tence that the Old Testament prophets had reached high levels of spiritual perfection and
in many instances had direct visions of God independently of the salvation-event of the
Incarnation." He further accuses Father Meyendorff of being motivated by "a complex
created in him" by charges among some Western scholars that "this kind of interpretation
... [by] ... the Greek Fathers ... of the Old Testament prophetic experiences" is an
example of "Greek Patristic Platonism" and "mitigates the significance of the ... person
of Christ," and thus of falling to an overstatement of the Incarnational and sacramental
mysticism of the Hesychasts. Father Romanides points out that "Father Meyendorff
makes use of a series of texts" from St. Gregory Palamas, "which he ... either mistrans-
lates or misinterprets," to make his unfounded case for a kind of "ineffable bodily union,"
in the Eucharist, between Christ and man that alone accounts for *theosis.* By such a claim,
as Romanides correctly observes, we must conclude that the Apostles on Mt. Thabor
were excluded from the deifying vision of Uncreated Light, as were the Prophets, whose
"vision of God in the Old Testament" St. Gregory Palamas defended. (See Romanides,
"Notes on the Palamite Controversy," Part II, pp. 236-246 *pass.*) It seems to me important that we place the Mysteries in Hesychastic spirituality precisely where I have (i.e., as
a central part of that spirituality), without risking the somewhat tortuous theological ela-
borations that Father Romanides correctly decries in Father Meyendorff's attempts to
respond to Western scholars whose views about Platonic influences on the Greek Fathers
are, as we saw in our discussion at the end of the previous chapter, largely invalid.

311. Chrysostomos, "Demonology in the Orthodox Church," pp. 52-53.

312. Metropolitan Hierotheos, *St. Gregory Palamas,* p. 137.

lure—, so the Church's Mysteries, combined with ascetic discipline, serve to cleanse the sullied mind; to restore, transform, and reorient human drives and desires towards spiritual ends; and to strengthen men and women in their struggle for enlightenment, deification, and the perfection for which, according to the Greek Fathers, they were created.[313]

The Deified Human Being

Since Orthodox psychotherapy addresses the human condition from within a medical model, we can rightly conclude our discussion of the cleansing of the mind and the "spiritual therapy" of the Hesychastic tradition by asking just what a human being who has been cured—i.e., deified, enlightened, or glorified by union with God—of the darkness which overcomes the *nous* when it is infected and afflicted with sin and subject to Satanic temptation (i.e., to all that takes one away from human perfection) is like. The obvious answer to our query is that Christ, the Divine Archetype, affords us, in His Perfect Humanity, a vision of all that man was created to be. The Saints, spiritual luminaries, and Fathers of the Church—these "small Christs within Jesus Christ"—also provide us with images of the transformed man and woman. Beyond such personages, who give us a glimpse of the full array of the unique (and diverse) personalities who constitute *restored man*, we can also say something about a few general psychological traits and attributes that portray the collective personalities of those who have succeeded in restoring the image of God within them and in fulfilling the Hesychastic vision of spiritual regeneration and rebirth.

An important distinction is made by Romanides between the Western contemplative mystic and the Hesychastic Saint, to whom the former is often compared. Whereas the Western contemplative is typically assigned to a cloistered existence—an austerity that can also be found in Orthodox monastic life, though in service to the aspirant's therapeutic regimen—and caught up in the ecstatic experience of God,

> Hesychastic spirituality makes it possible for one to go about engaging in his daily physical and mental activities while the noetic faculty [the cleansed essence of the mind], circumscribed within the body [within the heart] (and in another sense outside physical and discursive rational activity), is occupied un-

---

313. For further reading about the psychological dimensions of Hesychastic ascetic discipline as it is found specifically in the witness of the Desert Fathers, see Archbishop Chrysostomos, "Towards a Spiritual Psychology: the Synthesis of the Desert Fathers," *Pastoral Psychology*, Vol. 36, no. 4 (1989).

interruptedly in prayer alone, even during sleep.[314]

This active engagement with the world in the context of internal spiritual activity is, in the Hesychastic tradition, both the product of the cleansing of the mind (and concomitantly, the purification of the body) *and* the return of the *nous* to the heart (into communion with, and illumination by, Grace). It is the natural state of the human being. In this state, the body and soul act in harmony and the senses and emotions, redirected towards their original purpose and aims, act to dispose an illumined and deified individual towards the spiritual, inoculating him, as it were, against sin (the image of man represented, in part, by the *Theotokos*). Though not immune to sin, such an individual, living in "*to eschatologikon nyn*," or "the eschatological now," brings together the perfection of the future life with the restoration of man's goal of perfection in this life. Thus, one who has beheld Uncreated Light "is not awaiting the end of history and time," but "experiences now that which is expected after the Second Coming. . . . That is, the eternal embraces us at each moment of time. Thus, essentially we experience the past, the present, and the future in one constant unity."[315]

As a consequence of the broader perspective afforded by a life that brings the past, present, and future into a whole, into an *eternal moment,* those who have experienced divinization exhibit what the Hesychasts call the gift of *apatheia* or passionlessness. Of this gift or trait, Metropolitan Hierotheos says the following:

> Passionlessness, according to the teachings of the Fathers, is 'health of the soul.' If the passions are the illness of the soul, passionlessness is the healthy state of the soul. Passionlessness is the 'resurrection of the soul prior to the resurrection of the body.' . . . One who has rendered the senses pure, has lifted his mind above created things, has subdued all of his senses to his *nous,* places his soul ever before the Lord.[316]

Apatheia is not a state of indifference. Nor does it make an individual an insipidly passive person. Rather, it is a state in which one balances the present life against his or her experience of the next life, which is reified in one's encounter

---

314. Romanides, "Notes on the Palamite Controversy," Part II, p. 230.

315. Blachos, *Orthodoxe Psychotherapeia*, p. 23. This idea of an "eternal time" is also found in the concept of "liturgical time" in Orthodox worship, where the believer participates in a ritual event that brings together the temporal earthly and the eternal Heavenly and thus subtly alters and transforms the dimension of time.

316. *Ibid.,* p. 278.

with God and the internal life within the heart. Thus, an individual who is passionless is not without emotions and human longings, losses and triumphs, moments of sadness and moments of exhilaration, illness and health. It is simply that these things are placed in a larger context and the priorities of life are constantly established and reevaluated with reference to timeless and eternal goals and cognitions. Human psychology comes to encompass the worldly and the spiritual in conjunction, the former understood and reshaped through the latter. The enlightened man or woman, then, lives with an awareness of the sadness and imperfection of a *present* which is constantly informed by the joy and perfection of the *future:* accepting all that happens in the light of the Will of God, which illumines the heart and gives unity to all that has been, all that is, and all that will be in the eternal moment that is the New World of human perfection by Divine Grace.

Finally, lest by adequating Orthodox psychotherapy and the monastic practices of Hesychasm, I have left the impression that the methodologies of Hesychastic transformation are only for monks or nuns, let me immediately disabuse my readers of that thought. As Metropolitan Hierotheos clearly states, the Hesychastic life is one "that married people as well are able to live."[317] There is no part of the monastic life to which a layperson is not called, including even celibacy (as evidenced by the sexual abstinence of married couples during the many and long fasting periods of the Church). There is no ultimate distinction between monks and laypersons, or between so-called "white" and "black" clergy—i.e., between married and unmarried Priests (the Orthodox Church has had married clergy since Apostolic times). In the end, the ascetic practices of the Hesychasts are appointed to the whole body of believers. It is only in the degree of their application and practice that monastics and lay people differ in their spiritual efforts. In the end, the spiritual therapy of Orthodoxy is open to all men and women, and all people—from the ordained clergy to the Royal Priesthood of the people of God—are called to be cured and, to a greater or lesser extent, to be therapists, according to the ability and calling of each.

---

317. Metropolitan Hierotheos, *St. Gregory Palamas,* p. 32.

Chapter IV

The Clinical Applications of
Orthodox Psychotherapy

"You learn even, perhaps, how to tolerate the
evil in the world." *Andrew Solomon*[318]

This chapter is, in many ways, an epilogue to the foregoing chapters, since my purpose is not so much one of guiding the reader from the theory of Orthodox psychotherapy to its application, as it is to offer some comments and general caveats about that application. It is not my contention, of course, that religion and the mental health sciences do not have real points of convergence. In chapter one, above, I enthusiastically argue *that they surely do*. Nor do I wish to say that science and *Orthodox psychotherapy* have no points of convergence. I do not for a moment deny that some of the techniques of Hesychastic practice have parallels in treatment modalities used by psychologists and psychiatrists. Meditation and concentration, for example, have been used successfully to treat anxiety and stress.[319] There is some evidence, as well, that fasting can have an ameliorative effect even on the symptoms of disorders so serious as schizophrenia and depression.[320] Psychologists and psychiatrists have also argued that harmo-

---

318. Andrew Solomon, *The Noonday Demon: An Atlas of Depression* (New York: Scribner, 2003), p. 442.

319. In a recent article for the periodical *Time,* Lisa Takeuchi Cullen notes that scientific studies of meditation increasingly support the idea that quiet concentration and controlled breathing not only reduce stress, but may help "increase attention span, sharpen focus and improve memory." She cites the research of Sara Lazar at Massachusetts General Hospital (Harvard University's largest teaching hospital) which suggests that meditation may even affect the natural deterioration of portions of the cerebral cortex "that occurs with age." (Lisa Takeuchi Cullen, "How to Get Smarter, One Breath at a Time: Scientists Find That Meditation Not Only Reduces Stress But Also Reshapes the Brain," *Time,* January 16, 2006, p. 93.) For further reading about meditation and psychology, there is a fascinating and extensive body of literature linking Buddhist meditation with traditional Indian medicine and Freudian therapy. See, for example, the interesting work of M.W. Padmasiri de Silva, *Buddhist and Freudian Psychology*, 3rd edition (Singapore: Singapore University Press, 1992).

320. Chrysostomos, "Demonology in the Orthodox Church," p. 60.

ny between the body and mind has its curative effects. And what Orthodox psychotherapy says about the importance of love in the restoration of those suffering from psychological disorders is echoed even in popular writings about secular psychotherapy and its successes and failures.[321] However, it would be wrong and misleading to suggest that Orthodox psychotherapy has, as its *fundamental goal,* the treatment of psychological disorders or the specific concerns of the clinic and the secular therapist. In fact, none of my writings about Patristic psychology has ever, in a *direct way,* touched on my pre-monastic work as an academic psychologist and my research in the clinical application of social psychological theory and in Freudian and Jungian theory. Metropolitan Hierotheos, in his treatment of Hesychastic methodology, has *also* been careful to emphasize that "psychiatry and neurology are called to cure pathological anomalies" in behavior, while "Orthodox theology cures" the "*existential* dilemmas" of life and "the deeper causes that engender them."[322]

I might go even farther than Metropolitan Hierotheos and say that, at a global level, in most psychotherapeutic systems the ultimate purpose of the therapist is to restore the ego, the personality, or the self. Depending on the mode of therapy, this may involve, among other things, achieving an increased awareness of the subconscious inner dynamics of the individual (touching on developmental, sexual, and affective aspects of the psyche); the establishment of adaptive relations with others and the attainment of a positive sense of self-worth or self-esteem; or an encounter with existential issues that speak to the inner self or a sense of belonging and self-fulfillment, at a personal level, in the larger scheme of things. In terms of a holistic perspective on psychotherapy, in each of these cases there are both instances of concern for the relationship between the body and the mind (or the body and the soul) and circumstances in which spiritual matters arise. But the obvious and principal object of therapeutic attention still remains the treatment and emendation of human psychological ills. By contrast, the aim of Orthodox psychotherapy is, again, not the treatment of psychological maladies or various incidental symptoms of spiritual or existential malaise; its purpose is above all *spiritual,* and it addresses the concerns of secular psychotherapy only in a secondary sense and by way of curing specific spiritual ills as they are defined by the anthropology and soteriology of the Greek Fathers and Orthodox theology. Its primary aim is to unite the human being, body and soul, psychologically and somatically, to the Divine Energies and to restore the hu-

---

321. One such work is Andrew Solomon's bestseller, *The Noonday Demon, op. cit.*

322. Bishop Hierotheos, *Orthodox Psychotherapy,* Preface to the English edition, p. 138 (emphasis mine).

man *being* (using that term in its full ontic and noumenal sense) to a potential state of perfection, to the highest expression of humanity, to the brevet dignity of Divinity by Grace.

Not only is the aim of Orthodox psychotherapy different from that of secular psychotherapy, but also the techniques of treatment that the two may employ in common adventitiously are meant to have *very different consequences* and are predicated on much *different assumptions* about the constituent components of the psychosomatic structure of man. When the Hesychast speaks of the body and mind acting in concord, therefore, he does not mean what the secular psychologist means by mind-body harmonization. Moreover, Hesychastic therapeutic methods deal with more than incidental spiritual *images* and spiritual or religious *ideation;* they are immersed in something beyond cognition or the surprise of joy—beyond religious mystery and beyond the *mysterium tremendum* and *das ganz andere* of spiritual awe. Orthodox psychotherapy brings one *face à face* with the "otherly" in the form of the *facts of holiness,* with the *novus homo* and a new vision of what men and women can be. If psychotherapy can restore in us a sense of what we *are,* or even achieve, at times, the deontological end of knowing what we should *be,* Orthodox psychotherapy—in returning the mind to the heart and coordinating the spiritual essence of the mind with the discursive intellect and the body—reveals to man *deiform dimensions* of humanity that he has probably never imagined and ontological horizons that are submerged deep in the psyche and beclouded by the indurated accretions of mere existence. In the process of curing the mind as Orthodox psychotherapy envisions it, one moves past the mere restoration of mental health, and all that it entails, to deification and an endless, ineffable potential for growth and perfection. If the two processes of restoration are related, they are also separated by the encompassing splendor of spiritual renewal.

The Application of Hesychastic Methodology in Clinical Settings: Limitations and Dangers

Notwithstanding all that separates secular psychotherapy and Orthodox spiritual therapy, it is possible that psychological illnesses both of an existential kind and, perhaps, those stemming from physiological causes (e.g., from some neurochemical imbalance or deficit or from disease and trauma) can be benefited by the application of Hesychastic techniques.[323] After all, even the most naïve

---

323. As Metropolitan Hierotheos speculates, though Orthodox psychotherapy may even help an individual "protect himself from various physical illnesses," it "will be more

chemical determinist will admit that, just as neurochemicals can affect mental processes, so cognitive states and psychosomatic stimuli—and intervening spiritual concerns, I might add—can affect brain behavior. There are indeed, as I pointed out earlier, psychotherapists who claim to use Hesychastic methods effectively in treating patients. I have even read reports—albeit anecdotal in nature—of apparent "cures" by way of these disciplines. One of these is contained in a letter from a certain "A.G." (a graduate student in counseling psychology at the Franciscan University of Steubenville, Ohio) that appeared in the periodical, *Ekklesiastike Parembase* (Ecclesiastical input), published monthly in Greece by the diocese of Metropolitan Hierotheos. The writer reports the case of a woman who "told me that she was cured of schizophrenia with the help of an Orthodox priest who used the methods of Orthodox Psychotherapy (tis methodous tes Orthodoxou Psychotherapeias)."[324] The same woman apparently introduced "A.G." to the writings of Metropolitan Hierotheos, and specifically his work *The Illness and Cure of the Soul in the Orthodox Tradition* (*opus citatum*).

While I am fascinated by the clinical application of Orthodox psychotherapy, I am also disquieted by it; hence, my caveats about the dangers that it poses. First, I am very much an advocate of strict adherence to the scientific method in the evaluation of therapeutic modalities. As such, I find myself in complete concord with Columbia University Professor Eric Kandel, the Nobel prize-winning neurobiologist (and trained psychotherapist), about the need for better techniques of evaluation in psychotherapy and for placing psychotherapy "on as rigorous a level as psychopharmacology." I may lack Dr. Kandel's enthusiasm for the "revolution" in "psychopharmacological treatments"; however, I have no argument with him when it comes to holding psychotherapy to rigid scientific standards.[325] From that standpoint, the scant evidence that I have seen for the effectiveness of Hesychastic practices in secular psychotherapy—whether employed as a primary or supplemental method of treatment—is not luculent and is contained in clinical case reports that are not subject to the kind of scrutiny that arise from data gathered in controlled studies that adhere to good experimental design protocols, where clearly defined and operationalized independent and dependent variables can be subjected to careful statistical analysis and independently examined and appraised. In general, of course, psychotherapy has not un-

---

helpful to those who want to solve their existential problems." (*Ibid.*)

324. "Mia Epistole Gia ten 'Orthodoxe Psychotherapeia,'" (a letter about 'Orthodox psychotherapy')," *Ekklesiastike Parembase* (Ecclesiastical Input), No. 93 (November 2003), p. 9.

325. See his comments in an interview by Susan Kruglinski, "The Discover Interview: Nobel Laureate Eric Kandel," *Discover,* Vol. 27, no. 4 (April 2004), pp. 58-61, *pass.*

dergone this kind of scientific scrutiny, and its methods of evaluation, as Kandel opines, seldom rise to the level of good science. In that sense, what has been reported by those who attribute to Orthodox psychotherapy some modicum of therapeutic effectiveness is probably no less valid than what one sees in evaluative assessments of other forms of therapy. I say this, I should add, within the contexture of my earlier comments about what I consider the specific aims, proper scope, and limitations of Orthodox psychotherapy in its clinical application.

Second, given my concerns about the evaluative methods of psychotherapy, as well as the very limited clinical data about Orthodox psychotherapy, I have express and serious misgivings about unsubstantiated anecdotal evidence regarding the latter that may serve to perpetuate claims of cures by a "therapeutic method" which is neither designed for nor, in my personal opinion, always appropriate to the clinic. Whatever their effectiveness in such a setting, Hesychastic disciplines are open to abuse. Misunderstanding its purpose, the overzealous therapist might be led to believe that Orthodox psychotherapy can serve as a substitute for more traditional and established therapeutic modalities or for psychopharmacological (drug) intervention, which is often a very effective first course of action in treating serious psychological disorders. Hesychastic practices, which are *aimed at spiritual therapy*, are not a *substitute* for standard therapeutic modalities. I am not arguing, in saying this, that Hesychastic practices cannot *help* individuals to find relief from their psychological problems or to cope more effectively with them. As Dr. Kandel notes, with regard to the array of available therapies, "you might benefit from one, and I might benefit from another." It is difficult to predict accurately, as he observes, what is effective in treating psychological disorders: "[D]rug therapy is very effective," though "some patients . . . don't benefit from it"; some patients benefit from "drugs together with psychotherapy" and others from "psychotherapy by itself."[326] But such circumstances argue *against,* and not *for,* the indiscriminate or uncareful use of an untested spiritual regimen as a clinical tool *simply because it might work* and simply because psychotherapy still lacks a certain *scientific rigidity.*

At a broader level, I am also concerned with a trend in some circles within the Orthodox Church to equate certain *psychological illnesses* with disorders of a spiritual kind. This error is often accompanied by the unwarranted assumption that the spiritual treatments prescribed by the Church Fathers for such spiritual disorders somehow apply to these psychological illnesses, as well. I have written about this trend in reference to a book, *Heavenly Wisdom From God-Illumined*

---

326. *Ibid.,* p. 61.

Teachers on Conquering Depression,[327] which, while undoubtedly pious and quite well-meaning in its intentions, leads the reader to believe that *spiritual despondency*—or the "noonday demon," as St. John Cassian (d. 435) calls it— and *clinical depression* are the same thing:

> [T]his book . . . suggests that the language of spiritual life and medical psychology are necessarily identic; that is, that the depression (*melancholia*) often experienced in the course of ascetic and spiritual struggles is the same thing as clinical depression as a psychologist understands it. Admittedly, the symptoms often seem similar, but the etiology of each is more often than not quite different. Here . . . we come to the issue of superficial and specious associations between phenomena in spiritual therapy which . . . involve both noetic and dianoetic processes of a wholly unique and special kind. They are not phenomena [necessarily] attendant to the symptomology of psychological disorders. To imagine that they are is to misrepresent 'spiritual disorders' which frequently arise from demonic and psychic attacks and temptations and which, though they may play a role in psychological disorders, act and operate in a wholly different manner in the process of spiritual restoration than they do in the course of mental illnesses.[328]

The immediate danger in ignoring the kind of distinction that I make above is that of assuming, once more, that the method of cure applied to spiritual depression is applicable to clinical depression (which is a complicated disease that frequently involves accompanying physiological disorders or neurochemical imbalances that require drug treatment). In fact, the book in question contains a reference to the prevalence of depression in modern society as a consequence of religious disbelief and, oddly enough, the heresy of Chiliasm.[329] A gullible or naïve person suffering from clinical depression could easily come to the conclusion, therefore, that some change in religious belief or embracing some recommended religion might cure his or her psychological illness. Were such a conclusion to lead to the cessation of therapy or drug treatment, the results could

---

327. *Heavenly Wisdom From God-Illumined Teachers on Conquering Depression,* 2nd printing (Forestville and Platina, CA: St. Herman of Alaska Brotherhood and St. Paisius Abbey, 1998).

328. Archbishop Chrysostomos, "Scholarly Imprudence: Comments on Contemporary Trends in Orthodox Spiritual Writing and Byzantine Historiography," *Orthodox Tradition,* Vol. 21, no. 1 (2004), p. 10.

329. Abbot Herman, "Preface to the 'Caught Fishes,'" *Heavenly Wisdom,* p. 17. Chiliasm (Millinarianism or Millennialism), which dates to the second century, holds that before the end of the ages, Christ will return to earth and rule for a thousand years.

well be disastrous.

The tendency to confuse spiritual disorders described in the writings of the Church Fathers with psychological illnesses is not confined to misguided proponents of Orthodox psychotherapy. Andrew Solomon, whose book on depression and enlightening views on psychotherapy I cited earlier, traces the Christian understanding of depression back to St. Augustine and the medieval conviction that melancholy and its despair represented "a turning away from all that was holy" and were "evidence of [demonic] possession."[330] In fact, Solomon takes the title of his book from St. John Cassian's description of the demon of depression. It is my contention that the Greek Fathers, at least, speak of the demon of depression, as they do many other spiritual disorders, from outside the nosological categories of modern medicine. Nor do they, in my reading of their relevant writings, consider depression (mental illness), as Solomon asserts, a "punishment" that is "effective in redeeming" the sinful.[331] The Church Fathers do suggest that those who are mentally ill—as well as those who engage in sinful behaviors—are more susceptible to influence from demonic or evil psychic influences of Satanic provenance, though essentially because their illness prevents them from exercising effective vigilance against such influences. Thus, the Church ministers to the mentally ill, along with those who willingly or deliberately court psychic evil, in prayers of exorcism. But these ministrations are not meant to lift from them some putative curse or punishment by Divine wrath, but to free them from victimization by forces that seek their destruction, rather than their perfection. Just as Christianity introduced into the ancient world the "revolutionary idea" that "the infirm poor and other socially disadvantaged people were no longer to be despised" but "were to be honored,"[332] so individuals overtaken by evil—whether by their own machinations or the intervention of others—were to be treated by the curative intercessions of the Church. We see this clearly in one of the ancient prayers of exorcism written by St. John Chrysostomos, in which he invokes Christ, "the Physician of Souls and Bodies," entreating Him, as one Who "in every way beckons back" His "creature to Himself," to "help" and "restore" those "recumbent in pain" to "strength and health."[333]

---

330. Solomon, *The Noonday Demon*, p. 292.

331. *Ibid.*, p. 393.

332. Michael Dols, "Insanity in Byzantine and Islamic Medicine," in *Dumbarton Oaks Papers*, No. 38 (Washington, DC: Dumbarton Oaks Research Library and Collection, 1984), p. 141.

333. *Euchologion A: Hagiasmatarion* (Book of prayers I: Services of blessing) (Holy Mountain: Ekdosis Hieras Mones Simonos Petras, 2002), Part II, Section 3, "Prayers and Exorcisms by St. John Chrysostomos," pp. 188-189. Dols, acknowledging the "consider-

Orthodox Psychotherapy in Context: Addressing Its Integrity and Issues of Diversity and Universality

If I am both fascinated and disquieted by the prospects of using certain He-sychastic disciplines in secular psychotherapy, I am also pleased with the atten-tion of psychologists and psychiatrists to Orthodox psychotherapy, while having significant misgivings, at the same time, about the preservation of its integrity. When lifted out of its spiritual context and applied—whether in clinical settings or in the practices of other religious traditions—without sufficient reflection, Or-thodox psychotherapy can be quite easily distorted. This is precisely what Met-ropolitan Hierotheos writes in his intriguing comparative consideration of Or-thodox psychotherapy and Logotherapy:

> Orthodox psychotherapy is not an intellectual system that can be experienced
> and applied in an individualistic sense, but is realistic and pragmatic, because it
> is applied in its natural setting, which is the ecclesiastical community. . . . Fur-
> thermore, the fact that a person can be cured is inseparable from the existence
> of the Church, which is the Body of the God-Man Christ.[334]

As I have said, Orthodoxy psychotherapy is aimed at the restoration of the soul. Its aims were neither formed nor articulated in the language or realm of psycho-logy, and one should certainly not pretend, whatever its relevancy for secular psychotherapy, that this is not so. In an age not always sympathetic to religion, and sometimes banally ecumenical in its attitudes when it is, we too often lose sight of the importance of contextual integrity and the value of genuine diversity

---

able discrepancies" in the treatment of the mentally ill in Byzantium (p. 145), nonetheless cites a reference from the life of St. Theodosios the Coenobiarch (d. 529) to the Saint's fondness for something akin to "talk therapy" in "comforting" monastics who, "over zea-lous in their asceticism," were at times "led to derangement" and thus assigned to a "se-cluded section in his monastery" (*ibid.,* p. 146). In the *Life* of St. Theodosios, written by St. Symeon Metaphrastes (the Translator), we read, further, that St. Theodosios treated these beleaguered ascetics "as [though they were] his own children," showing them "ar-dent love" and an "affectionate disposition." It should be noted, too, that the locale as-signed to them in the monastery is described by St. Symeon, not merely as a "secluded" place; rather, he speaks of their having been assigned to a "topon hesychion te kai gale-non (a tranquil and serene place)." See St. Symeon Metaphrastes, "Bios kai Politeia tou Hosiou Patros Hemon Theodosiou tou Koinobiarchou (Life and conduct of our holy as-cetic father Theodosios the coenobiarch)," *Patrologia Graeca,* Vol. 114, col. 504A.

334. Metropolitan Hierotheos, *Hyparxiake Psychologia,* p. 188.

in our quest for religious universality.

The practices of Orthodox psychotherapy are inseparable from the absolutely Christocentric anthropology, cosmology, and soteriology of the Orthodox Church. If one is to draw from it various useful and effective therapeutic regimens, this should be done with a candid acknowledgement of the source and nature of those practices and with an objective, open-minded respect for the integrity of the wholeness of the tradition in which they have been applied for nearly two millennia. In a practical sense, I do not know whether, in the last analysis, these regimens will hold up to rigorous scrutiny as having real practical value outside of their spiritual context; i.e., whether, in fact, they will prove effective in dealing with psychological disorders. By the same token, I am not convinced that their partial or wholesale adoption as practices for spiritual rehabilitation are really meaningful outside the specific theological realm of Eastern Orthodoxy. There are many of us within the Orthodox Church who believe that the relevancy of our spiritual traditions, whether in psychology or religious life, lies not in the extent to which our beliefs and practices are interchangeable with those of non-Orthodox faith traditions, but in the integrity of our observance of a *way of life* that should serve to teach by example and not by the admixture and confusion of various traditions and practices. For me and other traditionalist Orthodox, true ecumenism (universalism) entails religious toleration, an appreciation of that diversity which respects the integrity of tradition, and the maturity to envision universalism within the confines of the language, ethos, and traditional mentality of strict observance.[335] This is not to say, as one Orthodox theologian

---

335. In this regard, the *Dictionary of the Ecumenical Movement* (ed. N. Lossky *et al.* [Geneva: WCC Publications, 2002]) contains an entry on the Old Calendarist traditionalists in the Orthodox Church (of whom I am one) as anti-Western "fundamentalists" of uncanonical provenance, portraying me in particular—much to my chagrin and embarrassment—as one who considers the ecumenical movement an "ecclesiastical heresy" and "demonic" (p. 486). Whereas words such as "heresy" and "demonic" are very often used as derisive epithets, in the vocabulary of the Hesychasts they are diagnostic terms, as I suggested in my discussion of Orthodox cosmology, anthropology, and soteriology in chapter two. That which in any way thwarts human deification is demonic; heresy is anything that contravenes or in any way dilutes or distorts the therapeutic system prescribed by the Orthodox Church; and the Church is a community of believers—the *New Israel*—who, of one accord theologically and spiritually, are undergoing, in the singular and peculiar Theanthropic Body of those united by a Mysteriological commonality, spiritual illumination and deification by Grace. Strict observance, singular focus, and attention to the integrity of historical tradition no more make an Orthodox traditionalist a bigot than they do an observant Jew. And when we as Orthodox speak diagnostically to those within our circles, we are not all speaking in the language of the religious bigot. I would like to

has written, that "our Orthodox counseling tradition" does not believe that "all people can be saved"; indeed, it teaches that we can all become, in following that tradition, "bridges of salvation for many others."[336] It is within this context that one should, from my perspective, approach Orthodox psychotherapy.

How Can Orthodox Psychotherapy Ultimately Benefit the Mental Health Sciences?

Given my repeated caveats about Orthodox psychotherapy, one might rightly ask, "What role, then, does Orthodox psychotherapy have in bringing together the mental health sciences and religion, and what role does it play in secular psychotherapy?" My answer is of necessity careful. To be sure, none of what I have said previously ineluctably rules out the possibility of a therapist applying various Hesychastic techniques in the course of traditional treatment modalities. I would simply suggest caution with respect to the dangers that I have enumerated. With Orthodox patients, of course, there is much less danger of abusing Orthodox psychotherapy, since its practices are more likely to form some part of their religious observance. In dealing with them, it is also far easier to involve a clergyman—and especially one knowledgeable about Hesychastic techniques—in the overall treatment regimen. If Orthodox psychotherapy has any place in secular psychotherapy, and if Hesychastic practices prove to be beneficial in the clinical setting (and I will reiterate that I am not sure that such is true, inasmuch as reliable data are still unavailable in what is, in any event, a field where meticulous evaluative procedures themselves are left wanting), my qualms about it as a mode of clinical therapy independent of its established aim and origin still persist. Nonetheless, this does not diminish my conviction about the important role of Orthodox psychotherapy in bringing together religion and the mental health sciences, and especially with regard to religious diversity and the treatment of Orthodox Christians.

More importantly, if we set aside the problematic question of Orthodox psychotherapy and its arguable efficacy as a therapeutic technique, we can draw from it philosophical insights and principles that can richly and freely inform the mental health sciences and imbue them, from within the Orthodox religious tradition, with lofty ends. For one thing, all of the virtues which we have said char-

---

make this clear, so that my language, in speaking of Orthodox psychotherapy, is in no way subject to misunderstanding.

336. Stephanos Koumaropoulos, "Mia Gerontissa Hegoumene Hos Symboulos (An eldress and abbess as counselor), *Ephemerios* (Parish priest), April 2004, p. 23.

acterize the divinized human being are virtues which all of us, Orthodox or non-Orthodox, divinized or not, religious or non-religious, can strive to attain. *Apatheia,* or the positive acceptance of blessings and adversity alike, not with Stoic quietude or in fatalistic resignation, but with a faith in the potential goodness of all mankind—this is an outlook that helps us to cope with life in all of its aspects. If we add to this the conviction that the human condition can be improved, that humankind is in the hands of a benevolent Creator Who wishes people freely to chose the higher good, and that the human being is capable of participation in the Energies of the Creator, the immediate peace that one gains touches the heart and suffuses the whole man, body and soul. If, by growing in such positive awareness, we come to grasp something beyond the mundane and gain an image of restored men and women, appropriating to ourselves a new world and a new grasp on life, we gain dimensions of selfhood that help to cure the anxieties and perplexities of life; and this not, perhaps, just at the existential level, but even at the level of cognitions, thoughts, and emotions.

I believe, too, that the love which characterizes Hesychastic man, as Father Romanides writes, obviates the idea (at least in the realm of religion) that "each believer has his own private relationship with God." And this fact has immense significance for the loneliness and existential abandonment that so often accompany psychological impairment. The destiny of man, as Orthodox psychotherapy sees it, is not a "motionless *eudaemonia* or self-fulfillment"; rather, man is called to a denial of self that leads to "complete and unselfish love": the kind of love that moved Moses in his "resistance to God's threat to destroy the people" with his offer to be blotted out of the "book of the living," if God would "pardon the sin of this people." Indeed, "perfect love . . . is even above our care for our own salvation when it concerns the salvation of others."[337] This sort of love, which binds us to our fellow man, is inspiring and renewing, restorative and essential. It is also something that subtly beckons us back to the spiritual life. The Nobel Laureate, Czeslaw Milosz, in his poem "There is No God," illustrates this point with irony bordering on enantiosis, contrasting, as he does, his stark, rejective title with lines that are actually a forceful theological affirmation:

If there is no God,
Not everything is permitted to man.
He is still his brother's keeper
And he is not permitted to sadden his brother,
By saying that there is no God.[338]

---

337. Romanides, *Ancestral Sin,* pp. 114-115 *pass.*
338. Czeslaw Milosz, *Second Space,* p. 5.

We see Milosz's affirmative rhetorical device unraveled in a simple aphorism from the Desert Fathers: "He who loves the Lord has first loved his brother, because the second is proof of the first."[339] In bringing all mankind into a single whole through love—man perhaps damned *alone* but saved *only together* with others, as the Russian writer Alexei Khomiakov (d. 1860) expresses this[340]—, this vision of men and women restored in love, a central aim of Orthodox psychotherapy, cannot help but enliven and bring new content to the core vision of secular psychotherapy and spiritual latitude to the mental health sciences.

Finally, I am convinced that my studies of Patristic psychology, as well as Metropolitan Hierotheos' revelation of the inner life of Eastern Orthodox Christianity through his books on psychotherapy, provide the non-Orthodox world with a supernal vision of human potential that elevates every man, facilitating in some mysterious manner the recovery of a profound nostalgia for perfection that has plagued and haunted humankind throughout recorded history. Somehow, at its very core, all religion tells us something about an ontological illness that afflicts us as humans. It also reminds us, when it is directed towards healthful restoration and transformation, that we are in need of being cured. And finally, by giving us an image of what human ontic health is, it calls us to new and curative dimensions and worlds of experience and presents us with archetypes of restoration. Above all, if science tells us about the world as it is, religion and the spiritual tell us about what the world can be, granting substance to our hopes and inner yearnings and yielding up ways of coping with what *is,* in anticipation of what *will be.* Hesychastic tradition combines all of these elements of religion *at its best* into an encounter with eternity, joining the present to the future in what I have called "the eschatological now." Vision is thus wedded to experience, giving essential content to religious observance and affording a foretaste of the perfection that awaits those who awaken in themselves that Divine spark that flickers in our nostalgia for a higher life—that spark of light, in the imagery of the Johannine Gospel, which "photizei panta anthropon erchomenon eis ton kosmon (lighteth every person that cometh into the world)" (St. John 1:9).

Orthodox psychotherapy, in aiming at virtues and behaviors that speak of the highest aspects of man—self-sacrifice for the sake of others, compassion, love, an abhorrence of bigotry and prejudice, disdain for hatred and resentment, non-violence and an inner love for peace, and the ecumenical openness to accept

---

339. St. John of the Ladder, *The Ladder of Divine Ascent,* revised edition (Boston, MA: Holy Transfiguration Monastery, 1978), p. 228.

340. See Rev. John S. Romanides, "Orthodox Ecclesiology According to Alexis Khomiakov," *The Greek Orthodox Theological Review,* Vol. 2 (Easter 1956), p. 66.

others for their differences and not in terms of what they are willing to betray to be what we are—, also tells us that man can be principled and courageous in humility, heroic in fighting with the weapons of peace, rich in his non-avariciousness, victorious over doubt in humble belief, and triumphant in weakness. While the methodology of Orthodox psychotherapy may not generalize to the clinic, its understanding of the potential within men and women speaks universally to the human heart. That *alone* gives hope to those who are suffering from psychological problems. That ideal *alone* can help one to cope with the present in the light of hope in the lambent future. And that *alone*, since it is a therapy for the patient and therapist alike, brings religion and science into intimate communication and dialogue.

Bibliography of Works Cited and Consulted

Adam, David. "Plan for Dalai Lama Lecture Angers Neuroscientists." *The Guardian,* July 27, 2005.

Adamides, Soteres K., M.D., Ph.D. *Therapeutike ton Pateron kai Psychoanalyse* (The therapeutics of the fathers and psychoanalysis). Athens: Ekdoseis A.E. Stamoules, 2002.

A.G. "Mia Epistole Gia ten 'Orthodoxe Psychotherapeia (A letter about 'orthodox psychotherapy')." *Ekklesiastike Parembase* (Ecclesiastical input), No. 93 (November 2003), p. 9.

Akakios, Archimandrite. *The Orthodox Christian and the Boundaries of Contemporary Medical Technology.* Etna, CA: Center for Traditionalist Orthodox Studies, 1996.

Aletti, Mario. *Psicologia, Psicoanalisi, e Religione* (Psychology, psychoanalysis, and religion). Bologna: Edizioni Dehoniana Bologna, 1992.

Armstrong, Karen. *The Battle for God: A History of Fundamentalism.* New York: The Random House Publishing Group, 2001.

Aslan, Reza. *No god but God: The Origins, Evolution, and Future of Islam.* New York: Random House, 2005.

Assagioli, Roberto. *Psychosynthesis: A Manual of Principles and Techniques.* New York: Hobbs, Dorman, *ca.* 1965.

Auxentios of Photiki, Bishop. *The Paschal Fire in Jerusalem: A Study of the Rite of the Holy Fire in the Church of the Holy Sepulchre.* Third edition. Berkeley, CA: St. John Chrysostom Press, 1999.

_____. "Notes on Pastoral Psychology." *Orthodox Tradition,* Volume XXIII, no. 1 (2006).

Avdeev, D.A. *Orthodox Psychotherapy.* Translated by Nicolas and Natalie Semyanko. Missionary Leaflet #E142. La Cañada, CA: Holy Trinity Mission, 2004 (http://www .fatheralexander.org/booklets/English/orthodox_psychotherapy_d_avdeev). Accessed January 3, 2006.

Baigent, Michael, Richard Leigh, and Henry Lincoln. *Holy Blood, Holy Grail.* New York: Delacorte Press, 2005.

Bakan, David. "Freud's Paper on Demonological Possession." Chapter nine in *Freud and Freudians on Religion: A Reader,* ed. Donald Capps. New Haven and London: Yale

University Press, 2001.

Balanos, Demetrios S. *Hoi Byzantinoi Ekklesiastikoi Syngrapheis* (Byzantine ecclesiastical writers). Athens: Apostolike Diakonia, 1951.

Balogiannes, Stauros I. *Psychiatrike kai Poimantike Psychiatrike* (Psychiatry and pastoral psychiatry [psychology]). Thessaloniki: Ekdoseis P. Pournara, 1986.

Barbatsoulias, Georgios. *He Neurose Kata Ten Karen Horney kai Hoi Anthropologikes Theoreseis tou Hag. Maximou tou Homologetou: Synkritike Melete* (Neurosis according to Karen Horney and the anthropological aspects [perspectives] of St. Maximos the Confessor: A comparative study). Athens: Ekdoseis Akritas, 2004.

Blachos, Archimandrite Hierotheos. *Orthodoxe Psychotherapeia: Paterike Therapeutike Agoge* (Orthodox psychotherapy: A patristic therapeutic regimen). Edessa, Greece: Hiera Mone Timiou Staurou, 1986.

_____. *Psychike Astheneia kai Hygeia: Dialogos.* (The sickness and health of the soul: A dialogue). Lebadeia, Greece: Hiera Mone Genethliou tes Theotokou, 1987.

Boa, Kenneth. *Augustine to Freud: What Theologians and Psychologists Tell Us About Human Nature (And Why It Matters).* Nashville: Broadman and Holman Publishers, 2004.

Bowman, Elizabeth S. "Integrating Religion into the Education of Mental Health Professionals." Chapter twenty-five in *Handbook of Religion and Mental Health,* ed. Harold G. Koenig. San Diego, CA: Academic Press, 1998.

Brown, Carolyn T. "Footprints of the Soul: Uniting Spirit with Action in the World." In *Dreaming the American Dream: Reflections on the Inner Life and Spirit of Democracy,* ed. Mark Nepo. San Francisco: Jossey-Bass (A Wiley Imprint), 2005.

Brown, Dan. *The Da Vinci Code.* New York: Doubleday, 2004.

Bulgakov, Sergei Vasilevich. *Nastol'naia Kniga dlia Sviashchenno-Tserkovno Sluzhitelei* (Desk reference book for sacred ecclesiastical servers). Third edition. Kiev: Tipografiia Kievo-Pecherskoi Uspenskoi Lavra, 1913.

Cabezas de Herrera Fernández, Ricardo. *Freud: El Teólogo Negativo* (Freud, the negative theologian). Salamanca: Universidad Pontificia de Salamanca, 1989.

Cambridge History of Later Greek and Early Medieval Philosophy. Edited by A.H. Armstrong. Cambridge: Cambridge University Press, 1967.

Cannon, Dale. *Six Ways of Being Religious: A Framework for Comparative Studies of Religion.* Belmont, CA: Wadsworth Publishing Company, 1996.

Carmignac, Jean. *The Birth of the Synoptics.* Translated by Father Michael J. Wren. Chicago: Franciscan Herald Press, 1987.

Cavarnos, Constantine. *Byzantine Thought and Art: A Collection of Essays.* Third print-ing. Belmont, MA: Institute for Byzantine and Modern Greek Studies, 1980.

_____. *Modern Greek Thought.* Second printing. Belmont, MA: Institute for Byzantine and Modern Greek Studies, 1986.

_____. *Immortality of the Soul.* Belmont, MA: Institute for Byzantine and Modern Greek Studies, 1993.

_____. *Pythagoras on the Fine Arts as Therapy.* Belmont, MA: Institute for Byzantine and Modern Greek Studies, 1994.

_____. *Fine Arts as Therapy: Plato's Teaching Organized and Discussed.* Belmont, MA: Institute for Byzantine and Modern Greek Studies, 1998.

_____. *Plutarch's Advice on Keeping Well.* Belmont, MA: Institute for Byzantine and Modern Greek Studies, 2001.

_____. *Aristotle's Theory of the Fine Arts: With Special Reference to Their Value in Education and Therapy.* Belmont, MA: Institute for Byzantine and Modern Greek Studies, 2001.

Cavarnos, John. *St. Gregory of Nyssa and the Human Soul: Its Nature, Origin, Relation to the Body, Faculties, and Destiny.* Edited and revised by Constantine Cavarnos. Belmont, MA: Institute for Byzantine and Modern Greek Studies, 2000.

Chraïbi, Sofia. *Jacques Lacan: Docteur de l' Église au Service de la Psychoanalyse* (Jac-ques Lacan: Doctor of the church in the service of psychoanalysis). Paris: François Xavier de Guibert, 2000.

Chrestou, Panagiotes K. "Neohellenic Theology at the Crossroads." *The Greek Orthodox Theological Review,* Volume XXVIII, no. 1 (1983).

Chrysostomos, Archimandrite [Bishop (of Oreoi; of Etna), Archbishop (of Etna)]. *The Ancient Fathers of the Desert: Translated Narratives from the* Evergetinos *on Pas-sions and Perfection in Christ.* Brookline, MA: Hellenic College Press, 1980.

_____. "Demonology in the Orthodox Church." *The Greek Orthodox Theological Re-view,* Volume XXXIII, no. 1 (1988).

_____. "Towards a Spiritual Psychology: the Synthesis of the Desert Fathers." *Pastoral Psychology.* Volume XXXVI, no. 4 (1989).

_____. Review of *The Winter Pascha: Readings for the Christmas-Epiphany Season,* by Thomas Hopko. *Orthodox Tradition,* Volume X, nos. 2&3 (1992).

_____. "Saint Gregory Palamas and the Spirit of Humanism: His Views on Tolerance, Human Dignity, and the Human Body." Paper presented at the Symposium on Byz-antine Humanism and Hesychasm, State University of New York at Albany, Fall term (1992). Reprinted in part in *Orthodox Tradition,* Volume XI, no. 2 (1994).

_____. "In Honor of St. Gregory Palamas." Translated by Bishop Auxentios, *Orthodox Tradition,* Volume XVII, no. 4 (2000).

_____. *Sfaturi Pastorale Ortodoxe din Perspectiva Psihologica* (Orthodox pastoral issues from a psychological perspective). Translated by Daniela Constantin. Iasi, Romania: Editura Universitatii "Alexandru Ioan Cuza," 2002.

_____. *Orthodox and Roman Catholic Relations from the Fourth Crusade to the Hesychastic Controversy.* Etna, CA: Center for Traditionalist Orthodox Studies, 2002.

_____. *Ortodoxia de Est si Crestinismul de Vest* (The orthodox east and the christian west). Translated by Deacon Father George Balaban and Raluca Balaban. Bucharest, Romania: Editura Universitara "Ion Mincu," 2003.

_____. "Scholarly Imprudence: Comments on Contemporary Trends in Orthodox Spiritual Writing and Byzantine Historiography. *Orthodox Tradition,* Volume XXIII, no. 1 (2004).

_____ and Hieromonk Auxentios. *Scripture and Tradition: A Comparative Study of the Eastern Orthodox, Roman Catholic, and Protestant Views.* Belmont, MA: Nordland House Publishers, 1982.

_____ with Hieromonk [Bishop] Auxentios and Hierodeacon [Archimandrite] Akakios. *Contemporary Eastern Orthodox Thought: The Traditionalist Voice.* Belmont, MA: Nordland House Publishers, 1982.

_____ with Thomas Brecht. "Jung and the Mystical Theology of the Eastern Orthodox Church: Comments on Common Ground." *Pastoral Psychology,* Volume XXXVII, no. 4 (1990).

_____ with the Reverend James Thornton. *Love.* Volume IV in *Themes in Orthodox Patristic Psychology.* Brookline, MA: Holy Cross Orthodox Press, 1990.

Col, José Juan del. *Psicoanálisis de Freud y Religión: Estado Actual de Ambigüedades por Resolver* (Freudian psychoanalysis and religion: The present state of the ambiguities to be resolved). Bahía Blanca and Buenos Aires: Instituto Superior "Juan XXIII" and Centro Salesiano de Estudios "San Juan Bosco," 1996.

Cullen, Lisa Takeuchi. "How to Get Smarter, One Breath at a Time: Scientists Find That Meditation Not Only Reduces Stress But Also Reshapes the Brain." *Time,* January 16, 2006

[Cyprian (Agiokyprianites), Archimandrite]. "On the Ascension of Our Lord," *Orthodox Tradition,* Volume XIX, no. 2 (2002).

Cyprian, Metropolitan of Oropos and Fili. "To Archetypon Mas kai He Diaphylaxis Apo Ta Eidola" (Our archetype and preservation from idols). *Hagios Kyprianos,* Volume IV, no. 329 (2005).

Diagnostic and Statistical Manual of Mental Disorders. Fourth Edition, Second printing. Washington, DC: American Psychiatric Association, 1995.

Dictionary of the Ecumenical Movement. Edited by N. Lossky *et al.* Geneva: WCC Publications, 2002.

Dols, Michael. "Insanity in Byzantine and Islamic Medicine." In *Dumbarton Oaks Papers*, No. XXXVIII. Washington, DC: Dumbarton Oaks Research Library and Collection, 1984.

Fauteux, Kevin. *The Recovery of Self: Regression and Redemption in Religious Experience.* New York and Mahwah, NJ: Paulist Press, 1994.

Florovsky, [Protopresbyter] Georges. *Bible, Church, Tradition: An Eastern Orthodox View.* Volume I in *The Collected Works of Georges Florovsky.* Second printing. Belmont, MA: Nordland Publishing Company, 1972.

_____. *Christianity and Culture.* Volume II in *The Collected Works of Georges Florovsky.* Second printing. Belmont, MA: Nordland Publishing Company, 1974.

_____. *Aspects of Church History.* Volume IV in *The Collected Works of Georges Florovsky.* Belmont, MA: Nordland Publishing Company, 1975.

_____. *Ways of Russian Theology: Part One.* Volume V in *The Collected Works of Georges Florovsky.* Belmont, MA: Nordland Publishing Company, 1979.

_____. *The Eastern Fathers of the Fourth Century.* Volume VII in *The Collected Works of Georges Florovsky.* Vaduz, Liechtenstein: Büchervertriebsanstalt, 1987.

_____. *The Byzantine Fathers of the Sixth to Eighth Century.* Volume IX in *The Collected Works of Georges Florovsky.* Vaduz, Liechtenstein: Büchervertriebsanstalt, 1987.

Freud, Sigmund. *Interpretation of Dreams.* Harmondsworth, England: Pelican Books, 1976.

Fromm, Erich, *Psychoanalysis and Religion.* London: Victor Gollancz Ltd., 1951.

Fuller, Andrew Reid. *Psychology and Religion: Eight Points of View.* Washington, DC: University Press of America, 1986.

Furedi, Frank. "Anti-Religious Hysteria" (online essay, 1/26/2006). *Spiked.* London: Signet House (http://www.spiked-online.com). Accessed January 24, 2006.

Gerasimos (Mikragiannanites), Monk. *Hebdomadarion: Parakleseis kai Chairetismoi tes Hebdomados* (Weekly service book: Supplicatory canons and salutations for the week). Holy Mountain [of Athos]: 1987.

Gill, Joseph. *Byzantium and the Papacy.* New Brunswick, NJ: Rutgers University Press, 1979.

Gordienko, N.S. "The Russian Orthodox Church Abroad." Chapter thirteen in *The Rus-*

sian Orthodox Church: 10ᵗʰ to 20ᵗʰ Centuries, ed. Alexander Preobrazhensky and trans. Sergei Syrovatkin. Moscow: Progress Publications, 1988.

Gordienko, N.S. and M.P. Novikov. "The Church Under the New Social Conditions." Chapter ten in *The Russian Orthodox Church: 10ᵗʰ to 20ᵗʰ Centuries,* ed. Alexander Preobrazhensky and trans. Sergei Syrovatkin. Moscow: Progress Publications, 1988.

Gregoriou tou Palama: Hapanta ta Erga (Gregory Palamas: Complete works). Edited by Panagiotes Chrestou. Thessaloniki: Paterikai Ekdoseis "Gregorios ho Palamas," 1981-1986.

Gregoriou tou Palama: Syngrammata (Gregory Palamas: Writings) Edited by P. Chrestou. Thessaloniki: Royal Research Society, 1966. Volume II.

Habra, Father George. "The Sources of the Doctrine of Gregory Palamas on the Divine Energies." *The Eastern Churches Quarterly,* Volume XII, no. 6 (1958).

Halligan, Frederika R. and John J. Shea. Introduction to *The Fires of Desire: Erotic Energies and the Spiritual Quest,* ed. Frederika R. Halligan and John J. Shea. New York: The Crossroad Publishing Company, 1992.

Handbook of Psychotherapy and Religious Diversity. Edited by P. Scott Richards and Allen E. Bergin. Washington, DC: American Psychological Association, 2000.

Heavenly Wisdom From God-Illumined Teachers on Conquering Depression. Second printing. Forestville and Platina, CA: St. Herman of Alaska Brotherhood and St. Paisius Abbey, 1998.

Hellenes Pateres tes Ekklesias (Greek church fathers). Edited by Panagiotes Chrestou. Thessaloniki: Paterikai Ekdoseis "Gregorios ho Palamas," 1984.

Hierotheos, Bishop of Nafpaktos [Metropolitan (of Nafpaktos; of Naupaktos and St. Blaise)]. *Orthodox Psychotherapy: The Science of the Fathers.* Translated by Esther Williams. Levadia, Greece: Birth of the Theotokos Monastery, 1994.

_____. *Hyparxiake Psychologia kai Orthodoxe Psychotherapeia* (Existential psychology and orthodox psychotherapy). Second edition. Lebadeia, Greece: Hiera Mone Genethliou tes Theotokou, 1997.

_____. *St. Gregory Palamas as a Hagiorite.* Translated by Esther Williams. Levadia, Greece: Birth of the Throtokos Monastery, 1997.

The Holy Bible: Containing the Old and New Testaments, Translated Out of the Original Tongues and With the Former Translations Diligently Compared and Revised (Authorized King James Version). New York: World Publishing, n.d.

Homans, Peter. Introduction to *Childhood and Selfhood: Essays on Tradition, Religion, and Modernity in the Psychology of Erik H. Erikson,* ed. Peter Homans. Lewisburg, PA: Bucknell University Press; London: Associated University Presses, 1978.

Hopko, Thomas [Father]. *The Winter Pascha: Readings for the Christmas-Epiphany Season*. Crestwood, NY: St. Vladimir's Seminary Press, 1984.

Hussey, J.M. *The Orthodox Church in the Byzantine Empire*. Oxford: Clarendon Press, 1990.

Irenaeus, St. *Proof of the Apostolic Preaching*. Translated by Joseph P. Smith, S.J. New York and Ramsey, NJ: Newman Press, 1952.

Jaffe, Lawrence W. *Liberating the Heart: Spirituality and Jungian Psychology*. Toronto: Inner City Books, 1990.

Jaffee, Martin S. *Early Judaism*. Upper Saddle River, NJ: Prentice Hall, 1997.

_____. "Mysticism and Monasticism: A Perspective from Judaism." Paper presented at the Spiritual Life Institute, St. Martin's University, Lacey, WA, June 2006.

Jaspers, Dr. Karl. *Allgemeine Psychopathologie: Ein Leitfaden für Studierende, Ärzte, und Psychologen* (General psychopathology: A guide for students, physicians, and psychologists). Berlin: Verlag von Julius Springer, 1913.

_____. *General Psychopathology*. Translated by J. Hoenig and Marian W. Hamilton. Volume I. Baltimore and London: The Johns Hopkins University Press, 1997.

Jefferson, Thomas. "Letter to Thomas Mann Randolph, Jr., July 6, 1787." In *The Papers of Thomas Jefferson*, ed. Julian P. Bond. Princeton: Princeton University Press, 1955.

John of the Ladder, St. *The Ladder of Divine Ascent*. Revised edition. Boston, MA: Holy Transfiguration Monastery, 1978.

Kertzner, Alexander. "Protestant Evangelical Theological Ideology: Its Conceptual Deficits Vis-à-Vis Palamite Apophatic Theology." *Orthodox Tradition*, Volume XXIII, no. 1 (2006).

Klemes (Agiokyprianites), Hieromonk. "Genuine Nobility: Monasticism and Sociability." *Orthodox Tradition*, Volume XXIII, no. 2 (2006).

Koenig, Harold G., M.D., Michael E. McCullough, Ph.D., and David B. Larson, M.D. *Handbook of Religion and Health*. New York: Oxford University Press, 2001.

Koumaropoulos, Stephanos. "Mia Gerontissa Hegoumene Hos Symboulos (An eldress and abbess as counselor). *Ephemerios* (Parish priest), April 2004.

Kruglinski, Susan. "The Discover Interview: Nobel Laureate Eric Kandel." *Discover*, Volume XXVII, no. 4 (April 2004).

Krumbacher, Karl. *Geschichte der Byzantinischen Litteratur: Von Justinian bis zum Ende des Oströmischen Reiches, 527-1453* (History of byzantine literature: From Justinian to the end of the eastern roman empire, 527-1453). Volume I. Reprinted. New York:

B. Franklin, 1958.

Laplanche, Jean and J.-B. Paontalis. *Lexilogio tes Psychoanalyses* (Dictionary of psycho-analysis). Translated by B. Kapsabeles, L. Chalkouse, A. Skoulika, and P. Aloupes. Fourth edition. Athens: Kedros, 1986.

Larchet, Jean-Claude. *Thérapeutique des Maladies Mentales: L'Expérience de l' Orient Chrétien des Premiers Siècles* (The treatment of mental disorders: The experience of the christian east in the early centuries). Paris: Les Éditions du Cerf, 1992.

_____. *La Divinisation de l'Homme Selon Saint Maxime le Confesseur* (The diviniza-tion of man according to St. Maximos the Confessor). Paris: Les Éditions du Cerf, 1996.

Larson, Susan S. "The Nearly Forgotten Factor in Psychiatry: What a Difference a Dec-ade Makes: The Twentieth Annual Oskar Pfister Award Address." Chapter four in *Faith, Medicine, and Science: A Festschrift in Honor of Dr. David B. Larson,* ed. Jeff Levin and Harold G. Koenig. New York: The Haworth Pastoral Press, 2004.

The Lenten Triodion. Translated by Mother Mary and Archimandrite Kallistos Ware. London and Boston: Faber and Faber, 1978.

Levin, Jeffrey S., and Linda M. Chatters. *Research on Religion and Mental Health: An Overview of Empirical Findings and Theoretical Issues.* Chapter three in *Handbook of Religion and Mental Health,* ed. Harold G. Koenig. San Diego, CA: Academic Press, 1998.

Lossky, Vladimir. *The Mystical Theology of the Eastern Church.* Reprinted. Crestwood, NY: St. Vladimir's Seminary Press, 1976.

[Mariam, Mother]. *The Life of the Virgin Mary, the Theotokos.* Buena Vista, CO: Holy Apostles Convent, 1989.

Maximovitch, Blessed Archbishop John. *The Orthodox Veneration of the Mother of God.* Translated by Fr. Seraphim Rose. Platina, CA: St. Herman of Alaska Brotherhood, 1987.

McCullough, Michael E., David B. Larson, and Everett L. Worthington. Introduction to "Mental Health," Section four, *Scientific Research on Spirituality and Health*, ed. David B. Larson, M.D., M.S.P.H., James Swyers, M.A., and Michael E. McCul-lough, Ph.D. Rockville, MD: National Institute for Health Research, 1998.

Meissner, William W., S.J., M.D. "So help me God! Do I help God or does God help me?" Chapter four in *Does God help? Developmental and Clinical Aspects of Relig-ious Belief,* ed. Salman Akhtar, M.D., and Henri Parens, M.D. Northvale, NJ, and London: Jason Aronson Inc., 2001.

Metallinos, Protopresbyter George. "The *Exomologetarion* of St. Nicodemos the Hagio-rite." *Orthodox Tradition,* Volume XIX, No. 1 (2002).

Meyendorff, [Father] Jean [John]. *Introduction à l'Étude de Grégoire Palamas* (Introduction to the study of St. Gregory Palamas). Paris: Éditions du Seuil, 1959.

_____. *A Study of Gregory Palamas.* Translated by George Lawrence. Second edition. Leighton Buzzard, England: The Faith Press, 1974.

_____. "The Metropolitinate of Russia: From Kiev to Moscow." Chapter eight in Aristeides Papadakis, *The Christian East and the Rise of the Papacy: The Church 1071-1453 A.D.* Crestwood, NY: St. Vladimir's Seminary Press, 1994.

Milosz, Czeslaw. *Second Space: New Poems.* Translated by Czeslaw Milosz and Robert Hass. New York: HarperCollins Publishers, 2004.

Model Curriculum for Psychiatric Residency Training Programs: Religion and Spirituality in Clinical Practice, ed. David B. Larson, M.D., M.S.P.H., Francis G. Lu, M.D., James P. Swyers, M.A. Rockville, MD: National Institute for Healthcare Research, 1997.

Molinos, Miguel de. *The Spiritual Guide Which Disentangles the Soul.* Edited by Kathleen Lyttelton. London: Methuen, 1907.

Muse, Stephen. Introduction to *Raising Lazarus: Integral Healing in Orthodox Christianity,* ed. Stephen Muse. Brookline, MA: Holy Cross Orthodox Press, 2004.

Nedelsky, (Rassaphore-monk) Sergey. "Palamas in Exile: The Academic Recovery of Monastic Tradition." M.Th. thesis, St. Vladimir's Orthodox Theological Seminary, 2006.

Nellas, Panayiotis. *Deification in Christ: The Nature of the Human Person.* Translated by Norman Russell. Crestwood, NY: St. Vladimir's Seminary Press, 1987.

Nicodemos the Hagiorite, St. *Hermeneia eis tas Epta Katholikas Epitolas* (Interpretation of the seven catholic epistles). Venice: 1806.

_____. *Nea Klimax* (The new ladder). Thessaloniki: Ekdoseis B. Regopoulou, 1976.

The Oxford Dictionary of the Christian Church. Edited by F.L. Cross and E.A. Livingstone. Third edition. Oxford: University Press, 1997.

Padmasiri de Silva, M.W. *Buddhist and Freudian Psychology.* Third edition. Singapore: Singapore University Press, 1992.

Papademetriou, George C. *Introduction to Saint Gregory Palamas.* New York: Philosophical Library, 1973.

Parakletike. Revised edition. Athens: Ekdoseis "Phos," 1987.

Patapios, Hieromonk and Archbishop Chrysostomos. *Manna from Athos: The Issue of Frequent Communion on the Holy Mountain in the Late Eighteenth and Early Nineteenth Centuries.* Oxford: Peter Lang Publishing, 2006.

Patrologiae Cursus Completus. Series Graeca. Edited by J.-P. Migne. Paris: 1857-1866.

Peck, M. Scott. *People of the Lie: The Hope for Healing Human Evil.* New York: Simon & Schuster, 1983.

Pentiuc, Eugen J. *Jesus the Messiah in the Hebrew Bible.* New York and Mahwah, NJ: Paulist Press, 2006.

Philokalia ton Hieron Neptikon (Philokalia of the sacred neptic fathers). Athens: Ekdotikos Oikos "Aster," 1974-1976.

The Philokalia: The Complete Text. Translated and Edited by G.E.H. Palmer, Philip Sherrard, Kallistos Ware, *et al.* London and Boston: Faber and Faber, 1979-1995.

Pincus, Harold Alan, M.D. Preface to *Handbook of Religion and Mental Health,* ed. Harold G. Koenig. San Diego, CA: Academic Press, 1998.

Psychoanalysis and Faith: the Letters of Sigmund Freud and Oskar Pfister. Translated by Erik Mossbacher and edited by H. Meng and E.L. Freud. New York: Basic Books, 1964.

Quasten, Johannes. *Patrology.* Volume I, *The Beginning of Patristic Literature.* Reprint. Westminster, MD: Christian Classics, Inc., 1983.

Robinson, John A.T. *Redating the New Testament.* London: SCM Press, 1976.

Romanides, Presbyter John Sabbas [John S., Rev. John S., Protopresbyteros Ioannes S.]. "Orthodox Ecclesiology According to Alexis Khomiakov." *The Greek Orthodox Theological Review,* Volume II (Easter 1956).

_____. *To Propatorikon Hamartema: Etoi Symbolai eis ereunan ton proypotheseon tes didaskalias peri Propatorikou Hamartematos en te mechri tou Hag. Eirenaiou Archaia Ekklesia en antibole pros ten katholou katheuthynsin tes Orthodoxou kai tes Dytikes mechri Thoma tou Akinatou Theologias* (Ancestral sin: Namely, contributions to the study of presuppositions concerning the doctrine of ancestral sin in the ancient church to the time of St. Irenaeus vis-à-vis the general direction of orthodox and western theology to the time of Thomas Aquinas). Athens: 1957.

_____. "Notes on the Palamite Controversy and Related Topics," *The Greek Orthodox Theological Review,* Part I, Volume VI (Winter 1960-61); Part II, Volume IX (Winter 1963-64).

_____. *Franks, Romans, Feudalism, and Doctrine: An Interplay Between Theology and Society.* Brookline, MA: Holy Cross Orthodox Press, 1981.

_____. "Orthodox and Vatican Agreement: Balamand, Lebanon, June 1993." *Theologia,* Volume VI, no. 4 (1993).

_____. *The Ancestral Sin: A Comparative Study of the Sin of our Ancestors Adam and Eve According to the Paradigms and Doctrines of the First- and Second-Century*

Church and the Augustinian Formulation of Original Sin. Translated by George S. Gabriel. Ridgewood, NJ: Zephyr Publishing, 2002.

_____. *Paterike Theologia* (Patristic theology). Thessaloniki: Ekdoseis Parakatatheke, 2004.

Rose, Father Seraphim. *Genesis, Creation and Early Man: The Orthodox Christian Vision.* Platina, CA: St. Herman of Alaska Brotherhood, 2000.

Rossis, Zikos. *Systema Dogmatikes tes Orthodoxou Katholikes Ekklesias* (System of dogmatics of the orthodox catholic church). Athens: 1893.

Russell, Jeffrey Burton. *A History of Heaven: The Singing Silence.* Princeton, NJ: Princeton University Press, 1999.

_____ and Douglas W. Lumsden. *A History of Medieval Christianity: Prophesy and Order.* New York: Peter Lang Publishing, 2005.

Setton, Kenneth M. *The Papacy and the Levant, 1204-1571.* Philadelphia: American Philosophical Society, 1976-1984.

Shchapov, Ya. N. "Christianity and the Church in the 12th-14th Centuries." Chapter three in *The Russian Orthodox Church: 10th to 20th Centuries,* ed. Alexander Preobrazhensky and trans. Sergei Syrovatkin. Moscow: Progress Publications, 1988.

The Septuagint with Apocrypha: Greek and English. Translated by Sir Lancelot C.L. Brenton. Third reprinting. Peabody, MA: Hendrickson Publishers, 1990.

A Select Library of the Nicene and Post-Nicene Fathers of the Christian Church. Edited by Philip Schaff and Henry Wace. Second series, reprint. Grand Rapids, MI: Wm. B. Eerdmans Publishing Company, 1991.

Softas-Nall, Basilia (Lia). "Reflections on Forty Years of Family Therapy, Research, and Systematic Thinking in Greece." Chapter ten in *Global Perspectives in Family Therapy,* ed. Kit S. Ng. New York and Hove, East Sussex: Brunner-Routledge, 2003.

Solomon, Andrew. *The Noonday Demon: An Atlas of Depression.* New York: Scribner, 2001.

Soloveitchik, Rabbi Joseph B. *Halakhic Man.* Translated by Lawrence Kaplan. Philadelphia: The Jewish Publication Society, 1991.

Sophocles, "Antigone." In *Fabulae,* ed. A.C. Pearson. Reprint. Oxonii: E Typographeo Clarendoniano, 1975.

Stein, Murray. "From Freud to Jung and Beyond: Turning Points in Psychoanalytic and Religious Thought." Chapter one in *The Fires of Desire: Erotic Energies and the Spiritual Quest,* ed. Frederika R. Halligan and John J. Shea. New York: The Crossroad Publishing Company, 1992.

Stein, Rob. "Prayer Doesn't Aid Recovery, Study Finds." *Washington Post*, March 31, 2006.

Stephanou, E. "La Coexistence Initiale du Corps et de l'Âme d'Après Saint Grégoire de Nysse et Saint Maxime l'Homologète." *Échos d'Orient*, Volume XXXI (1932).

Storr, Anthony and Anthony Stevens. *Freud and Jung: A Dual Introduction*. New York: Barnes and Noble Books, 1998.

Symeon the New Theologian, St. *The Sin of Adam and Our Redemption*. Number two in the series, *Orthodox Theological Texts*. Platina, CA: St. Herman of Alaska Brotherhood, 1979.

Szasz, Thomas. "Psychotherapy: Medicine, Religion, and Power." In *Philosophy, Religion, and Psychotherapy: Essays in the Philosophical Foundations of Psychotherapy*, ed. Paul. W. Sharkey. Washington, DC: University Press of America, 1982.

Telepneff, Reverend Gregory and Archbishop Chrysostomos. "Hellenistic and Patristic Thought on the *Kosmos* and Man in the Greek Fathers." *Orthodox Tradition*, Volume VIII, Nos. 3&4 (1996).

Theokletos Dionysiates, Monachos. *Ho Hagios Gregorios ho Palamas: Ho Bios kai he Theologia Tou 1296-1359* (St. Gregory Palamas: his life and his theology 1296-1359). Thessaloniki: P. Ginnoules, K. Tsolerides, G. Dedouses, 1984.

Theologie in Dialog Mit Freud und Seiner Wirkungsgeschichte (Theology in dialogue with Freud and the history of his impact). Edited by Kurt Lüthi and Koloman N. Micskey. Vienna, Cologne, and Weimar: Bühlau Verlag, 1991.

Thielman, Samuel B., M.D., Ph.D., "World View in Global Perspective." Chapter eleven in *Handbook of Spirituality and Worldview in Clinical Practice*, ed. Allan M. Josephson, M.D., and John R. Peteet, M.D. Washington, DC and London: American Psychiatric Publishing, Inc., 2004.

Torelló, Juan Bautista. *Psicoanálisis y Confesión* (Psychoanalysis and confession). Translated by José Luis Martín. Second edition, revised. Madrid: Ediciones Rialp, S.A., 1974.

Tsirpanlis, Constantine N. *Introduction to Eastern Patristic Thought and Orthodox Theology*. Collegeville, MN: The Liturgical Press, 1991.

Vlachos, Archimandrite Hierotheos. *The Illness and Cure of the Soul in the Orthodox Tradition*. Translated by Effie Mavromichali. Levadia, Greece: Birth of the Theotokos Monastery, 1993.

Ware, Timothy. *The Orthodox Church*. Second edition. London and New York: Penguin Books, 1993.

Weaver, Andrew J. "Mental Health Professionals Working With Religious Leaders."

Chapter twenty-four in *Handbook of Religion and Mental Health,* ed. Harold G. Koenig. San Diego, CA: Academic Press, 1998.

Webb, Eugene. *The Self Between: From Freud to the New Social Psychology of France.* Seattle and London: University of Washington Press, 1993.

_____. "Religious Thought and the Psychology of World Views [2006]." TMs (photocopy).

Wilson, William P. "Religion and the Psychoses." Chapter eleven in *Handbook of Religion and Mental Health,* ed. Harold G. Koenig. San Diego, CA: Academic Press, 1998.

Winquist, Charles E. "Lacan and Theological Discourse." Chapter one in *Lacan and Theological Discourse,* ed. Edith Wyschogrod, David Crownfield, and Karl Raschke. Albany, NY: State University of New York Press, 1989.

Wood, Clement. *How to Psycho-Analyze Your Neighbors.* Girard, KS: Haldemann-Julius Co., n.d. (Little Blue Book #1344).

_____. *A Psycho-analysis of Jesus.* Girard, KS: Haldemann-Julius Co., 1926. (Little Blue Book #1071).

Yannaras, Christos. "Theology in Present-Day Greece." *St. Vladimir's Theological Quarterly,* Volume XVI, no. 4 (1972).

_____. "The Distinction Between Essence and Energies and Its Importance for Theology," *St. Vladimir's Seminary Quarterly,* Volume XIX, no. 4 (1975).

_____. *The Freedom of Morality.* Translated by Elizabeth Briere. Crestwood, NY: St. Vladimir's Seminary Press, 1984,

Young, Tony R., "Psychotherapy with Eastern Orthodox Christians." Chapter four in *Handbook of Psychotherapy and Religious Diversity,* ed. P. Scott Richards and Allen E. Bergin. Washington, DC: American Psychological Association, 2000.

Index

About the Author

The Most Reverend Chrysostomos, Exarch in America for the Synod of Old Calendarist Greek Orthodox Bishops under Metropolitan Cyprian of Oropos and Fili, completed his doctorate in psychology at Princeton University, his graduate studies in Byzantine history at the University of California, and his theological training at the St. Gregory Palamas Monastery in Etna, California, where he is a Senior Research Scholar at the Center for Traditionalist Orthodox Studies. He has held professorial appointments in psychology at the University of California and Ashland University, an adjunct professorship in Eastern Christian thought at the Ashland Theological Seminary, and a visiting professorship in Patristics and the psychology of religion at the Theological Institute of Uppsala University in Sweden. As a Fulbright Scholar in Romania, he also taught Byzantine historical theology, business ethics, consumer behavior, and the theology of Orthodox art and architecture at the University of Bucharest, the Alexandru I. Cuza University, and the Ion Mincu University of Architecture and Urbanism. He later served for a year as Executive Director of the United States Fulbright Commission in Romania.

His Eminence is a former fellow of the National Endowment for the Humanities and a former visiting scholar at the Harvard Divinity School, the Graduate Theological Union, Berkeley, the Henry M. Jackson School of International Studies at the University of Washington, Seattle, and, under the sponsorship of the Marsden Foundation and at the invitation of Bishop Kallistos (Ware), at Pembroke College, Oxford University. He completed research for the present volume as the David B. Larson Fellow in Health and Spirituality at the John W. Kluge Center of the United States Library of Congress. His latest book, with Hieromonk Patapios, is *Manna From Athos: The Issue of Frequent Communion on the Holy Mountain in the Late Eighteenth and Early Nineteenth Centuries* (Oxford: Peter Lang Publishing, 2006).